T0366148

GLIMPSES OF
GOD'S
GRACE

THE EXTRAORDINARY LIFE OF AN ORDINARY GUY

Lt Col William M. "Spike" Jones
(USAF, retired).

WESTBOW
PRESS
A DIVISION OF THOMAS NELSON
& ZONDERVAN

Scripture taken from the Holy Bible, NEW INTERNATIONAL
VERSION®. Copyright © 1973, 1978, 1984 by Biblica, Inc.
All rights reserved worldwide. Used by permission. NEW
INTERNATIONAL VERSION® and NIV® are registered trademarks
of Biblica, Inc. Use of either trademark for the offering of goods or
services requires the prior written consent of Biblica US, Inc.

WestBow Press books may be ordered through booksellers or by contacting:

WestBow Press
A Division of Thomas Nelson & Zondervan
1663 Liberty Drive
Bloomington, IN 47403
www.westbowpress.com
1 (866) 928-1240

Because of the dynamic nature of the Internet, any web addresses or
links contained in this book may have changed since publication and
may no longer be valid. The views expressed in this work are solely those
of the author and do not necessarily reflect the views of the publisher,
and the publisher hereby disclaims any responsibility for them.

Any people depicted in stock imagery provided by Thinkstock are models,
and such images are being used for illustrative purposes only.
Certain stock imagery © Thinkstock.

ISBN: 978-1-4908-4532-6 (sc)
ISBN: 978-1-4908-4533-3 (e)

Library of Congress Control Number: 2014913618

Printed in the United States of America.

WestBow Press rev. date: 12/31/2014

CONTENTS

CONTENTS

U. S. AIR FORCE HYMN

Lord, guard and guide the men who fly
Through the great spaces of the sky;
Be with them traversing the air
In darkening storms or sunshine fair

Thou who dost keep with tender might
The balanced birds in all their flight
Thou of the tempered winds be near
That, having thee, they know no fear

Control their minds with instinct fit
What time, adventuring, they quit
The firm security of land;
Grant steadfast eye and skillful hand

Aloft in solitudes of space;
Uphold them with Thy saving grace.
O God, protect the men who fly
thru lonely ways beneath the sky

ABOUT THE AUTHOR

Lt. Col. Spike Jones (USAF retired) is a US Navy brat who served 25 years as an USAF officer, instructor pilot, squadron commander and fighter pilot after graduating from the USAF Academy. He is an award-winning aviator. He lives with his award-winning wife of 34 years and their children in Carrollton, Virginia. After retiring from the Air Force n 2005, Colonel Jones suffered a massive, near-fatal stroke leaving him paralyzed on the left half of his body. He wrote this, his first book, from a wheelchair in an assisted living facility in Hampton, Virginia.

A *Christian fighter pilot?!* Is that even possible? Sure; I'm one. In my career, I met many more. You will, too, if you read on!

If you count my four years at the USAF Academy (Why wouldn't you? They were the four toughest years.); I served in the Air Force for twenty nine years. The Air Force was fifty eight years old in 2005 when I retired. That means I served in the USAF for half of its existence. I don't think anyone from my sister services can make that same claim. I absolutely loved serving in the Air Force. Loving what you do for a living is a true blessing from above. In my case, I sometimes couldn't believe they paid me to do the awesome things you'll read about later. They even paid me bonuses to keep on doing it.

WHY THIS BOOK – WHY NOW?

In May of 2013, due to reasons you'll read about later, I moved into the Chamberlin Hotel in Hampton, Virginia. The Chamberlin is a senior living facility offering various levels of care and assistance as their clients require. I wound up living in a small apartment there for a year.

As the "new kid in town," everyone was interested in my background and drilled me with questions. After learning of my unique high school experience and my long career flying in the Air Force; more than one fellow resident told me, "You should write a book." So I did. I decided to structure it as I see it. My life, as extraordinary as it is, is so solely because of a series of blessings from God. By detailing my flying career, I hope to attract those interested in military aviation (who isn't?) and reveal God's gracious plan of salvation to someone who might not be tempted to pick up a Bible.

DEDICATIONS

- To my Godly mother.

- To the Pastors, lay leaders, and Sunday school teachers of America's churches.
- To the military family.
- To the soldiers, sailors, and airmen of America's armed forces.
- To Shirley; my incredible wife, convincing proof of how much our God loves me.

- To my children; Laura, Jacob, and niece, Katie.
- To my cousin, Anita
- To the memory of my friends, Milton Heath (Kathy Farmer's father) and Colonel Pat Murphy Precious in the sight of the Lord is the death of his saints. (Psalms 116:15, NIV)
- To Harvest Fellowship Baptist Church (HFBC) in Smithfield, Virginia (think ham.)
- To the Adult II Bible Study Class at HFBC led by Bill Myers.
- To Rob and Kathy Farmer.
- To the PT Divas at Belle Harbour Physical Therapy.
- To the Genesis Rehab Staff at the Chamberlin Hotel.
- To the staff at the historic (and definitely not haunted) Chamberlin Hotel.
- To the residents of the Chamberlin.
- To the participants, volunteers, and quadrupeds of the Horses Helping Heroes Project. Please consider a donation to this wonderful program at horseshelpingheroesproject.com.

WHAT THIS WORK IS

My story based solely on my recollection. At 56 years old, my recollection is beginning to elude me. My sincere hope is that any reader, who, like me, doesn't aspire to big things, like I didn't, realizes the Creator of the universe and everything in it has a plan for you (Psalms 139:16).

Your plan was set in motion before He said the first, "Let there be…" and with His help, you really can do all things (Philippians 4:13). If you accept (And why wouldn't you? It's all true!) that a 130 lb. band geek did what's recorded in this work, you'll get it: With God, nothing is impossible! (Luke 1:37, NIV). I'm living proof of this.

WHAT THIS WORK ISN'T

100% historically accurate. I'm giving it my best shot with the residual brain damage I have as a result of the stroke I survived six years ago. But consider this:

I'm never wrong. I thought I was once, but I was mistaken.

Professionally edited. I just couldn't handle that big expense. This may have been a mistake. I relied on my spell-checker and public education for grammar and punctuation. I apologize for errors that escaped my attention and hope they aren't too distracting.

DISCLAIMER

There is no provision in the Ten Commandments which says Honor thy mother and father *as long as they live*. So even though my father has gone to heaven before me; I am to continue honoring him. In this work, you may (will) read what could be construed as insults directed at our Army and Navy. How can I honor my father and insult the service to which he devoted thirty years of his life? Any derogatory remarks directed toward my *sister* services are mere manifestations of good-natured, inter-service rivalry. I know this for a fact:

When it's time to go to war – It's One Team – One Fight and nobody does it better than we do!

WHAT I BELIEVE

- The Bible is the word of God, written by men inspired by God's Holy Spirit, and preserved through the centuries by God.
- I'm confined to this wheelchair because God wants a closer relationship with me. It's like He said, "Son, sit down and pay attention! You and I need to talk!" The stroke certainly got my attention; and I've been sitting for six years, now, but more importantly, it caused me to rely on Him daily. It's made me mindful of Isaiah 40:31 which says:

They who wait on the Lord shall renew their strength; they shall mount up on the wings like *Eagles,* (emphasis, mine), they shall run and not grow weary, they shall walk and not grow faint. (NIV)

Ultimately, everyone should know this happened to me for His glory. This is sometimes hard to see now, but I have faith it is true.

- The Bible is authoritative and reveals absolute truth (Yes, there is such a thing.) to those wise enough to study it.

I believe what the Bible says about Jesus Christ:
- He was born of a virgin; making Him fully human (except for our sinful nature) and fully God.
- Thirty-three years after his miraculous birth, he *willingly* sacrificed himself on a Roman cross to make atonement for our sins; restoring the possibility of a relationship with God, who is so exceedingly holy, he cannot associate with us in our inherited sinful state.
- He rose from the dead on the third day, like He said He would, and later ascended to heaven from where He will soon return.
- He performed all the miracles recorded in the scriptures. These events were foretold centuries before they happened.
- Like John Calvin, I believe the Bible teaches God chose those who would come to a saving faith in Christ before creation. I believe God is absolutely sovereign. As creator of time, space, matter, energy, and the laws governing them, He has complete control over it all.

- God is never surprised. According to Romans 8:28, "In all things God works for the good of those who love Him, who have been called according to His purpose." (NIV) Not only is He involved in everything, He works it all out for the *good* (even the bad stuff) of His believers.

• I believe America has been the preeminent military, economic, and technological power on earth for the last two hundred and thirty-seven years because she has been blessed by God, because of the faith of her founders. They weren't perfect but examination of the first few years of our nation's struggle for independence bears witness to the fact that we only survived our founding through the miraculous grace of God. Read David McCullough's *1776* and you will be amazed that our unprepared, ragtag armed forces defeated the most powerful military on the planet to become an independent nation. Divine intervention is the only explanation. We may not be a "Christian nation" but there is no denying the fact that America and her form of government were founded on Judeo-Christian principles found in the Bible.

• I believe God will soon begin withholding His favor if we continue thumbing our national nose at Him. We celebrate what He detests. We gorge ourselves on raw sewage at the movie theaters and in our homes via television. The music we grew up on was vile but nothing compared to the explicit, violent, depraved ear manure to which our kids listen today.

We removed prayer from schools and Christian

symbols from our public places. We legalized, condoned, and played accomplice in the death of millions of unborn Americans (60 million and counting at a rate of thousands per week since Rowe v. Wade) - all in the name of women's rights. Abortion is not a civil rights issue. It is a moral issue! We allowed organizations, like the ACLU, to turn the first amendment on its head. Separation of Church and State (a phrase found nowhere in our founding documents) has been shamefully warped to hyper-secularize a once God-fearing people. The first amendment is meant to keep government out of religion – not to keep religion out of the public arena.

Want to learn how our government is supposed to work? Make time to read the U.S. Constitution; then follow up by reading The Federalist Papers. They were written to explain our form of government to the masses to help ratify our constitution. These are all the text our high schools need to teach government in America's classrooms.

Don't make the mistake, like many I've heard (including our president), of referring to the USA as a democracy. *We are not a democracy*! We are a Republic which uses democratic processes to elect our representatives.

- I believe we are in the "end of days." Christ will return very soon like He said He would.
- I believe the only event left to occur before His return is the completion of His church. When the last person God chose before creation comes to a saving faith

in Jesus Christ and accepts His gracious offer of salvation – the church will be complete and He will return to collect His bride (How the Bible refers to His church). Could one of you readers be that person? I hope so. I'm ready! Is everyone else? You had better get ready! Read on to discover *why* and *how*. You could be a hero in heaven if you're **the one** to get Jesus back down here. A recurring theme in the Bible is *the last will be first*. So if you're the last to seek and receive salvation through Christ, you'll be first in line at the Pearly Gates. That would be so cool!

WHAT I DON'T BELIEVE

- I don't believe in luck, karma, fate, or coincidence. If what goes around, comes around; it's because God ordained it that way. I say again, God is sovereign. He is in absolute control and does whatever pleases Him. *Everything* that happens; good or bad, as assessed from our miniscule perspective in our fallen sinful state, does so in accordance with His perfect plan and purposes.
- I don't believe God allowed my stroke as punishment for a sin or wrong-doing or a right-not doing [knowing what you ought to do and not doing it is sin(James 4:17).]. Someone was brutally punished two thousand years ago for all my sins (past and future). Jesus Christ took 100% of my punishment. It would be unjust for me to be punished now for a sin debt which was paid in full on the cross. God's justice is perfect. The Bible teaches when I accepted Christ's free gift of salvation

as a boy in Jacksonville, FL; I was clothed in His righteousness. (II Corinthians 5:21 & Isaiah 61:10) Many theologians refer to this as the Great Exchange (our sin for His righteousness). So get this:

When God looks at me now, He sees Jesus' righteousness, not my messed up attempts to be good enough to deserve His favor. His grace is awesome! It doesn't get better than that! – Jesus did it all; I do nothing but believe, and we both look the same to God (like twin brothers!) and we'll both spend eternity in paradise together. Paradise is how Jesus described heaven to the repentant thief on the cross beside Him. Heaven must be an incredible place, if Christ, who created every place in the universe, singles heaven out as paradise. The Bible says that no one can even conceive how wonderful the place is which God is preparing for those He loves. (I Corinthians 2:9, NIV)

- I don't believe there is a government conspiracy to cover up UFO sightings, crashes, or visitations.
- I don't believe the earth was visited by aliens in ancient times and shared their technology enabling humans to do things astonishing to us now. Just because we can't figure out how the ancients did it; doesn't mean ET taught them.

Science says the earth is 4.5 billion years-old - Nonsense. Science needs it to be this old to support its flawed theories.

- I don't believe Charles Darwin's *theory* on the origin of the species (evolution) holds water. It is taught to our children as undisputed fact. This is a lie. The theory of evolution is highly disputed! Our children should be familiar with the theory because of its profound impact on our culture, but they need to know the truth – the theory is highly disputed and doesn't stand up to scientific scrutiny. Why don't our schools teach our children the truth?! Political Correctness is going to bite us in the backside some day!

GRACE 101

- Simply put, grace is unmerited or undeserved favor – receiving something of benefit you don't deserve, didn't pay for, work for, or even ask for. Applied to me; glimpses of grace look like repeated blessings from God, throughout my lifetime for no other reason than it pleases Him to bless me. But not because of anything I did. By nature, God is loving, generous, and eager to bless. GRACE writ large is remembered by the acrostic: God's Riches At Christ's Expense. (Get it?) Why me? Because, He loves me. Why does He love me? I don't know, I'm not very loveable.
- But it's not just me. Ever look up John 3:16? Why not? Please go do that now, I'll wait… Now you know. It's not only me; it's everyone in the world which includes *everyone*. Pretty cool, huh? You should read the Bible more often. It's full of coolness like that.

CHAPTER I
GENESIS

Unlike comedian Steve Martin, I was not born a poor black child. Instead, I was born to a US Navy Sailor and his wife in the small, southern Alabama, town of Bay Minnette in the fall of 1957. (Read: Sputnik baby) Dad was stationed at Baron Field.

My given name is William Michael. My parents wanted to name me after my father's youngest brother, Billy, but they didn't want to call me William, or any of its derivatives, so they called me by my middle name, Michael or Mike. Twenty eight years later, in Montgomery, Alabama, Phil Finch bestowed "Spike" on me and it's been Spike ever since.

Both my parents were born and raised in Atlanta during the Great Depression. My paternal grandfather ran moonshine from family stills in the Florida panhandle to the speakeasies on the gulf coast. By contrast, my maternal grandfather was a Baptist preacher who drove electric streetcars in Atlanta after he retired from the ministry. Mom graduated salutatorian of her high school class while Dad stopped going to high school early, to get on with life. In 1949, he enlisted in the Navy. As I understand his plan; he intended to join up for a single hitch to learn how to work on diesel engines. He then planned to get out and work at the Chevrolet plant in Atlanta like others in his family. He re-enlisted after that first hitch to buy a green convertible. He retired in 1979 as a Lieutenant Commander.

My parents married in 1950. When I arrived on the scene, I had two older siblings, Rick and Karen. The Navy then sent us west. Our family of five, with three children under the age of six, left southern Alabama for southern California.

After leaving AL for CA, 1958

In San Diego, we lived in base housing on Coronado near NAS (Naval Air Station) North Island. I have few memories of San Diego. However, I do remember the renowned, unfortunate hamster incident:

In our small, second-floor apartment home, my brother, Rick had a pet hamster (or was it a guinea pig?)

(Does anyone really know the difference?) I was holding the rodent in question and Rick wanted whatever it was back. I wasn't immediately forthcoming in surrendering it, so a chase ensued with me out front holding the critter securely in my wee little hands at the end of my outstretched arms just barely out of reach of my faster big brother. I soon ran out of places to escape. My parents' bedroom had a small balcony with a rail a little over armpit high. That's where I found myself; on my toes, armpits on the rail, with my arms stretched out to keep the critter out of Rick's long reach. Somehow the rodent liberated itself from my grasp and began its free-fall sans parachute at 32 feet/sec^2 to the pavement below. Sometimes, gravity is not your friend. Technically speaking, the varmint converted its potential energy (height) into kinetic energy (motion) which was converted to lethal force upon its rapid deceleration with the pavement. Problem solved. I win! Rick can't reach it, now! Remember f = ma from high school physics? Neither did the hamster; or was it a guinea pig? Regardless, this was exactly what passed through my keen young mind. Then I pondered; if a hamster and guinea pig were both dropped from the same balcony at the same time, which one would hit the pavement first?

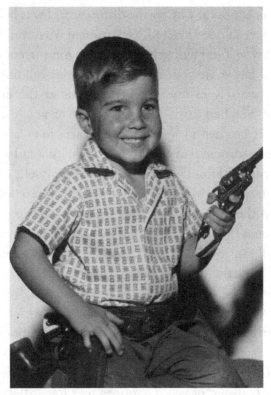

Already showing a fascination with weapons in 1959

I blame the whole incident on Rick. He should have known better than to trust me with his pet. It's too bad his pet rodent wasn't a flying squirrel!

About the time of the unfortunate hamster incident, a baby boy was born to another young Navy family on Coronado. George and Jean Jacobs welcomed their second child, and only son, to the world. They named him Larry. The Jacobs family later plays a significant role in my life; but first, the Navy has a few more moves for these two families. Next up – Texas.

CHAPTER II

KINGSVILLE

After North Island, Dad was assigned to NAS Kingsville, near the vast Kings Ranch in south central Texas. Kingsville holds memories of family campouts at Garner State Park in a large green canvas tent purchased at Sears. I attended Rick's Little League Baseball games where Dad umpired. I went to see my first movie, *Flipper*, with Rick and Karen. We stayed seated to watch its second showing.

I clearly remember the day President Kennedy was assassinated in Dallas:

I was outside riding my bike, a recently acquired skill. When I went back in our small white house on East Johnston Street, Mom who had been vacuuming was stopped in front our television crying. I felt anger when she told me what happened.

In Kingsville; I attended Harvey Elementary, my first of three first grade classes. But most significantly, in March of 1961; while the Joneses looked forward to the coming south Texas heat, without air conditioning; the Jacobs, stationed at NAS Patuxent River, Maryland, brought daughter number two into to the world. They named her Shirley.

Eons ago, God ordained that nineteen years later,

Shirley Jacobs would become Shirley Jones. I believe God knit her together in Jean's womb for that purpose. Before the Jacobs left Pax River, they added one more daughter, Teresa, to the nest. That's three Daughters and one son. I neglected to mention child number one, Janet, born about a month before me.

Let's get these families together. I'm getting there but first, they need to move some more.

In Kingsville, Dad was accepted into the Limited Duty Officer program; in which Noncommissioned Officers attend Officer Candidate School (OCS) to receive commissions as Ensigns followed by so many years in their respective career fields. Their ranks were limited to Commander and their total service time was limited to thirty years.

Dad left us in Kingsville to attend OCS. We rejoined him in Pensacola, Florida where he attended Aircraft Maintenance Officers School. We lived in a hotel on the beach in Gulf Breeze. I attended number 2 of 3 first grade classes at Gulf Breeze Elementary on Hwy 98. I survived sunburns and the chickenpox.

With family in tow, brand new aircraft maintenance officer, Ensign J.R. Jones, headed east to join VA-34(navy jargon for fixed-wing attack squadron 34) based at NAS Cecil Field on Jacksonville, Florida's west side. But VA-34 wasn't at Cecil; it was stashed aboard the USS Saratoga, an aircraft carrier in the Mediterranean. The family settled into a small house on Joffre Drive in the Normandy Village neighborhood; while Dad continued on to join his ship.

With the moving van still in front of the house, a kid about my size came over to check for potential playmates in the new family. This kid rang our door bell to see if I wanted to play. I had yet to acquire a taste for unpacking boxes (I never did.), so I went him and met his family two doors down on Joffre Drive. Dang! Three sisters!

That February day in 1965, I met my future wife. I was seven, she was three.

We mutually agreed to delay dating until after puberty (whatever that is). Then we'd see about taking our relationship to the next level (one without coodies). I didn't meet my future father in-law that day, though. Dad met him before me.

Chief George "Jake" Jacobs was an F-4 mechanic in a VF (fighter) squadron on board the Sara.

The Jones family, 1965

Mom wrote Dad about his new neighbor in VF-31 so one afternoon Dad went to the hangar deck to find where VF-31 worked on their planes. He shouted, "Is there a George Jacobs around here?!" From inside the intake of a nearby Phantom came the Virginia-accented reply, "Who the heck (or something like that) wants to know?!" Then a wiry jet mechanic with dark brown wavy hair and a tan, weathered face slid out of the F-4 to meet his new neighbor and shipmate, Ensign Jim Jones.

Jake looked every bit his rank but Dad, who was about Jake's age wore the rank of a twenty-something year-old kid. By coincidence (disregard, I forgot I don't believe in those!)One of Dad's other-younger brothers (Dad was the oldest of four brothers and one sister), Harold, was also on the Sara. While in the port of Naples, Italy, where I would later attend high school; Dad, Harold, and Jake went into the city for dinner. At the conclusion of the meal, Dad excused himself to visit the men's room.

The Jacobs Family, 1963. My future bride is sitting on Jake's lap.

During his absence, Jake and Harold conspired to stick the new officer with the check. They left quickly and returned to the ship. Dad and Jake remained friends and golfing buddies until their deaths about a year apart over fifty years later. Before I start killing off too many characters, let's return to Jacksonville. But first- some levity to cheer everyone up:

I have always been in search of jokes clean enough to tell my mother, a PK (preacher's kid). In our vulgar culture, this has been challenging. I recently saw a televised interview of Larry the Cable Guy. The usually vulgar Larry actually told a joke you can tell your mother and I can share in a Christian-themed book. It went something like this:

Following a battery of extensive medical tests a man met with his doctor to discuss the results. The doctor told him, "I have bad news and worse news." The man asked for the bad news first. The doctor told him, "I'm afraid you only have twenty-four hours to live." Astonished, the man asked, "Doc, What could possibly be worse news than that?!" The doctor replied, "I forgot to call you yesterday."

CHAPTER III
A KID IN JACKSONVILLE

Normandy Village was a great place to grow up. There were many kids in the neighborhood and great Florida weather. I walked to Normandy Village Elementary (3 of 3), until third grade when the rules allowed me to ride my bike. Several other boys near my age became good buddies and participated in backyard campouts, flashlight tag in the evenings and capturing lightning bugs (fire flies) which were plentiful in the warm-weather months. We'd also compete with our bikes; building ramps and attempting the longest jump ala Evil Kneval, or seeing who could cat walk the farthest. Cat walking our bikes was the feat of pulling the front wheel off the ground and balancing while pedaling on the rear wheel alone. This practice stopped when 10-speed bicycles came on the scene. Then we competed for speed and ventured off on long distance rides.

I-295 circumnavigates Jacksonville. After it was completed; but before it opened to traffic, we rode our 10-speeds on it from Westside south around to Orange Park. We also went through a skateboard phase; first with home-made models and later on store-bought, Santa delivered boards. When they repaved Monteau Drive, we enjoyed the smooth fast ride on the fresh asphalt down the hill from Joffre to where the creek passed under the street. In short, we were typical American kids loving life and having fun.

During fall and winter we played football until dark. In the spring and summer we played baseball in an empty field in the neighborhood. Corot Drive was our out outfield. A well-hit ball rolled all the way down to Joffre. Outfielders had to hustle before it disappeared down a storm drain. A typical summer day consisted of fitting as many ball games as we could into our busy schedules. Sometimes we'd break for lunch or ride to the 7-11 for a coke or an Icee. If too hot, we played in someone's sprinkler. If raining, we played in the rain unless there was lightning. A heavy down pour often overwhelmed the drainage system and flooded Joffre. This was even better; we rode our bikes in the rain and splashed through the deep puddles.

THE EMPTY POOL

Occasionally, Mom drove me out to the Officer's Club pool at Cecil Field, where I practiced my diving skills. One trip to the pool remains forever etched in my memory because my life was being cut tragically short.

We arrived before the pool opened so no one was in it yet. I was going to be the first! I already had my swimsuit on. I went through the locker room, skipping the required pre-swim shower like everyone else. When I emerged into the bright, Florida sunlight there was still no one in the pool and no lines at the diving boards. I walked as quickly as possible, taking care not to break stride into a run drawing the wrath of the lifeguards. I arrived at the base of the high dive unmolested by the embarrassing lifeguard whistle and began my climb up the ladder confident that every eye around the pool was on me. Is that kid really going to dive from way up there? Naugh, he'll probably just jump off the end. Why isn't he wet? Did he skip the shower like me? I took my position on top of the board and tried to look good for the TV cameras. I quickly filed through my extensive diving repertoire and selected the classic swan dive. What it lacked in technical difficulty; it made up for in sheer beauty and artistry, leaving them hungry for more. I began my march down the board with my head held high. Approaching the end of the board, I jumped up taking care to point my toes and raise my extended ended arms high over my head. I came down on the end of the board and it compressed down as it should to rebound me high into the air which it did. With straight legs, pointed toes, and arched back, I rose into the sky assuming the classic swan pose. Now to descend elegantly; and cleanly enter the water, leaving only a rip on its surface. But it was not to be. I looked down from the heavens and my heart seized with fear and horror. *There was no water in the pool!* Apparently, in my juvenile haste to be first; I hadn't noticed the reason no one was swimming in the pool was because *there was no water in it! You can't swim without water!* All these years later, my damaged brain clearly remembers seeing the bold black lane stripes against the light blue-painted cement bottom and the rusty *drain grate, but I couldn't see any water*! Fortunately, my youth meant the life that flashed before my eyes was brief. For an instant, I felt a kindred bond with Rick's hamster;

or was it a guinea pig? I guess I'll never know. Now gravity was not my friend. I hoped the cameras were getting all this. Don't look, Mom! You lifeguards will be *so* fired after this! My eyes were as wide as saucers when I hit the water which was invisible to me because no one was in the pool to disturb the water's surface. Ouch! That stung! But at least I was alive. ***And I was the first one in the pool!*** Heart racing, I swam to the nearest ladder and climbed out having executed a first class face-flop. Yep, I meant to do that. This is why they spray little jets of water onto the surface of the pool at diving competitions.

Back in the safety of my neighborhood, after a day of baseball or football, when it started to get dark or I heard Dad's distinctive whistle, I headed home, stopping to wash my filthy feet outside before I went in for dinner.

The area behind our backyard was heavily wooded with a small creek running through. – Perfect for catching tadpoles, hunting snakes with BB guns, and picking wild blackberries, the size of your thumb.

While on Joffre Drive, I joined the Cub Scouts Pack 363 (Mom was my Den Mother.) I rose through the ranks to Weeblo and transitioned to Boy Scout Troop 363(Dad was one of my Scout Masters.) I loved Scouting. I would like to say I made Eagle Scout. But if nothing else, Scouts are honest. - I didn't. I stopped two merit badges shy of Life (one rank below Eagle) when we left the country.

In troop 363, our Tenderfoot initiation pranks went way beyond Snipe Hunting. Ever been branded, bitten by a rattle snake, or jumped off a railroad bridge into an alligator-infested river in the dark? No one was ever hurt with these pranks, but they sure thought they were!

Our adult leaders scared the bigeezees out of us once: We camped near the Florida- Georgia line at the St. Mary's River. In the woods we discovered an old, weathered headstone by a huge oak tree marking an old grave which had sunken down as they will do when their contents decay. The headstone marked the grave of Caroline Hightower. We gathered around her grave one evening while, Mr. Gregory told us Caroline's story. According to Mr. Gregory, Caroline and her brother were part of the Underground Railroad. The siblings were caught red-handed smuggling slaves across the river. Caroline was hung on the spot from a branch of the moss-laden oak tree in front of us while her brother dug her grave underneath his dangling sister. He swore revenge on his sister's murderers.

Great story- a little spooky, like we wanted; there's the river, there's the tree, there's the grave. It all fit. We didn't know our assistant scoutmaster, Mr. Hughes, lay on the grave covered with leaves, moss and other ground clutter. He was invisible. At just the right moment, he came up off the grave with a shout and we almost wet our pants (maybe some did!) Lessons learned in Scouts helped me years later at Survival training.

In Jacksonville, I decided to follow Rick's lead and learn to play the trumpet. So with his tarnished, hand-me-down horn, I took beginning band the summer before I entered Joseph Stilwell Junior High School in 1970.

In teaching music over my junior high school years; Band Director, Horace Marsh taught me as much about self-discipline, commitment, teamwork, and leadership as any sports team, organization, or training program

I attended in all my 29 years in the military. He did the improbable by taking a band which earned an Unsatisfactory rating at state contest (a rare occurrence, but self-esteem issues with children weren't a priority back then; (You stink, Get over it!) to an Excellent rating *the following year* with a third of the band being inexperienced seventh-graders like me.

By my ninth-grade year, Mr. Marsh had taught every one of us in the symphonic Band from beginning students in our respective instruments. At state contest that year, we earned Superior ratings (highest possible) in every category and a Superior rating overall. Mr. Marsh made us feel like were a cut above. (Easy for him, we were!) He publically recognized band members excelling outside the band room. But he wasn't all rainbows and unicorns.

While riding my bus home one afternoon, I realized I had forgotten about an after-school rehearsal for an upcoming concert – my first as a member of the Symphonic Band. I showed up at the normal Band period the next day expecting a good chewing out; but instead, Mr. Marsh matter-of-factly told me I would not play in the concert. I was required to attend, but my participation as a musician was no longer required. Harsh! He might just as well have stabbed me through the heart with his baton. I never missed another rehearsal! Mr. Marsh's style was contagious. Whenever an individual or section nailed a difficult piece they had been working on, the whole band applauded and cheered. We about blew the roof off when Pam Carter played the piccolo descant to *Stars and Stripes Forever* to perfection.

One afternoon during my ninth-grade year, I knew

something big was up when I heard Mr. Marsh exclaim, "There goes another one!" He was talking to my parents outside his office door. "Did we get our orders?" I asked them. "Yes," Mom replied. "We're going back to Naples." My parents were stationed there in the early fifties. Karen was born there.

So instead of accompanying my band mates, close friends, and girl friend to the recently opened, Ed White high school, with air conditioning and carpeting, I was heading overseas to an unknown high school probably built by the Romans.

I was first bitten by the love bug at Stilwell. Her name was Lindy. She was blonde, pretty, and sat first chair in our Saxophone section. She was also a majorette and captain of the girls' basketball team - quite the catch.

At fifteen, we thought we had it all worked out. We'd be faithful through high school on separate continents. Then I'd go to the Naval Academy. Upon graduation, we'd marry and live happily ever after. (In the Navy?!) Thank God, he had a better plan. I had a new girlfriend within two weeks of arriving in Naples. So much for Lindy's plan! You might have already figured out we lived in Jacksonville for nine years. This is unusual for a Navy family. More grace? I think so.

Family life growing up in Jacksonville wasn't a Norman Rockwell painting but it was close enough for me. Mom took the kids to church every Sunday while Dad slept in. We came home to find him in his boxers with the Sunday paper spread out all over the dining room table. He didn't have anything against church. He was churched as a kid and came to a saving faith in Jesus

Christ as a young man. He and, his sister, Voncile, were in a Gospel quartet that performed on the radio. Before his death in 2008, he regularly attended First Baptist Church of Orange Park, Florida where he sang in the choir.

He used to tickle me when he, Jake, and I played golf. If he used the wrong club or hit the ball wrong sending it soaring near vertical, He'd say, "Don't touch it, Lord, it's a two-stroke penalty!" Then, when he crushed a drive or sank a long put, he attributed it to "clean living" and "singing in the choir." Of course, where attended church and what he did there made no difference as to where he is right now. It was that profession of faith in Christ as a young man that guaranteed his lofty address forever.

Someday I will join him there because as a boy in Jacksonville, I made the same profession of faith in Jesus Christ while attending Hyde Park Baptist on Lane Ave. I later moved over to Westside Baptist in Normandy Village just in time to get plugged into the youth group along with Karen.

When Dad was in Vietnam, he was able to take some time off from the war to visit an Armed Forces recreational area on Cam Rahn Bay. He took sailing lessons and quickly learned to love the sport. One of the first things he did on his return after beating his kids for a year's worth of infractions; was purchase a sailboat.

He bought a used, nineteen-footer with a small cabin. She needed some TLC which she received in our carport on Joffre Drive. She had a lot of mahogany trim which we (Dad) pulled out and varnished. Dad also trailered her out to Cecil Field's paint barn and gave her a beautiful emerald green hull.

One of our first adventures in her was a forty-mile trip from the marina at NAS Jacksonville to the home of a Navy buddy in the small river town of Palatka, Florida. Forty miles is a long way to go in a nineteen-foot sailboat against the current. The normally docile St. Johns River was tossed a bit because the huge Category 5 Hurricane Camille was coming ashore in Mississippi. Her outer bands reached clear across north Florida to Jacksonville. We had gusts to forty knots and five-foot swells in a river! That trip always seemed to come up for discussion whenever we were together. Later, Dad taught me to sail on his boat and one of my life-long passions was born.

Another passion born in Jax was my love of music. Perhaps; it is because their first big hit, *Close to You*, coincided with my summer in beginning band, The Carpenters have been my favorite group since 1970. Lindy gave me my first Carpenters Album. Over the years, I purchased only a handful of their albums. The rest were gifts. One way or another, I collected them all. Over recent years, I've recollected all those albums on CD. On cruise; Dad purchased high quality stereo equipment. I loved to put on a Carpenters album, lie on the living room floor, slip on the headphones, and bask in the beauty of their tight harmonies, incredible orchestral arrangements, and featured instrumental solos. In my opinion, Karen Carpenter was the finest female vocalist of our time. She also played a mean drum set. I was grieved to learn of her death in February of 1983. I regret never having the opportunity to attend a concert.

One unusual childhood memory of growing up in Normandy Village involved my school's Fall Carnival held every year in the parking lot in front of the school on Herlong Road. It included all the classics: corndogs, cotton candy, popcorn, and candied apples, plus games to win cheap little, cheesy prizes.

Shortly after one of these carnivals, I attended a PTA meeting and won a raffle for a turkey just in time for Thanksgiving. After the meeting, I was led back to the cafeteria's kitchen where I expected to receive a nice frozen Butterball.

But no, they gave me a white, 22 lb, live turkey in a wooden crate. I called home get a ride for my new pet and me. We let the bird live in our utility room until we could figure out what to do with it. Fortunately,(for us, not so much for the bird) there was a poultry processing facility not far from our home that transformed the turkey into something more like I expected to take home after winning the raffle.

I suspect Christmas is a special time for every kid. I was no exception. We typically, we had a live tree (usually a Scottish Pine) illuminated with the medium, C-9 size lights and adorned with glass ornaments, garland, and shiny silver aluminum icicles placed on one at a time. A manger scene with all the essential characters set out somewhere in the living room. My parents brought it back from Italy.

Outside, I helped Dad string the large C-7 size lights on the roofline on the front of the house. Then we outlined the large picture window on the front porch with miniature lights, nicely framing the Christmas tree on display inside the living room. We often wrapped the front door with green or red foil paper and hung an artificial wreath on it.

To me, it was absolutely beautiful and I couldn't wait for dusk each evening so I could flip the switches to turn it all on. I also looked forward to church after Thanksgiving when Christmas carols worked their way into the hymn line-up. Then there was the very popular, *Charlie Brown Christmas* on Channel 4 (CBS) and *Rudolph the Red-nosed Reindeer*.

On cruise; Dad had recorded hours of Christmas music on his reel-to-reel tape deck, so we always had Christmas music playing in the house.

On Christmas Eve our family tradition was to go out for barbeque and then drive around to look at Christmas lights. Back then gas was on around 30 cents per gallon. Then it was back to our own beautifully decorated house for one last look at all those presents under the tree before we tore into them the next morning. Of course; with three snoopers in the house, Rick, Karen, and I, pretty-much knew everything under there. Sorry Mom, but thanks for the challenge. Our mom-made stockings had been hanging as decorations for a while so with that essential task complete, we went to bed to endure the slowest night of the year. This time of year was an adventure for me. Between the time the tree went up to Christmas Eve (about a week), I practiced quietly sneaking out of bed, down the hall, and into the living room where I'd turn the tree lights on and sit and watch a while and quietly examine any package whose contents was still to be determined. If only it would snow!

I've borrowed some of these traditions and added a few unique to my wife and children. Seeing Christmas observances in other countries was interesting. We picked and choose from those, too; for example, we have a German blown-glass pickle ornament that we hang on the tree. The first child to find it gets to open a present. We also have a large nail we hang on a beefy branch to remind us the baby in the manger was born to be nailed to a Roman cross thirty-three years later. The first Christmas was necessary to make the first Easter to happen. And it's the empty tomb that makes all the difference in eternity for all of us.

If you've read Maria Von Trapp's book (the inspiration for *The Sound of Music*) you discovered that Austrian Catholics' Christmas tradition includes a visit by the Christ Child (Krist Kindle) bringing gifts for the family. I find it interesting how this tradition morphed its way to the American tradition of Kris Kringle bringing gifts on Christmas Eve. While we're on the subject of Christmas – I was home this past weekend to attend church and host our Sunday school class's annual Christmas party. While admiring the job Shirley did decorating our house and Christmas tree; I realized the trappings of our modern materialistic Christmas can reflect the true essence of the holiday, if we look for it.

The Christmas tree for example, is an evergreen, representing the everlasting life Christ offers. The gifts underneath the tree represent not only the gifts delivered to the Christ child by the Magi, but the incredible gift God gave mankind by clothing himself in flesh and stepping into our world as a helpless baby in a livestock feeding trough. Our tree has hundreds of miniature white lights, each representing Jesus as the light of the world. We cover our tree with little bits of white plastic artificial snow. This reminds me that Christ's blood shed thirty-three years later washed away our sins making us *Whiter than Snow*. This was the hymn we sang when our daughter Laura, whom you will meet later, went forward at our church in Hinesville, GA to make public her decision to be a Christian.

We have stockings for each of us hanging from the mantle in our living room. In order to receive gifts; the stocking must be open at the top. Like the stocking, our hearts must be open to receive the gift God offers through his son born that first Christmas

Before we leave Joffre Drive – More about Dad. There was no doubt in the Jones household as to who was boss. Mom let Dad think he was.

Let me be clear – Dad was king of his castle on Joffre Drive. We referred to his recliner as "the throne." He sat at the he sat at the head of our table with Mom to his right. (The place of honor) We carried on the southern practice of: "Yes sir-no sir and "Yes ma'am-no ma'am. My children were taught the same.

We used to have great three versus one wrestling matches in the living room, where Dad pretended to work hard at defeating his children. Dad was great fun and liked scare the daylights out of you. On a trip to the Appalachian Mountains one year, we were bedded down for the night in a rented camper. It was a dark and stormy night. (Cue creepy pipe organ music) We had just finished talking about the wild animals living in those woods. Karen sat up to look out one of the camper's small windows. In the darkness, Dad stealthily slipped his hand between her face and the window. His timing was perfect.

The lightning flashed, he made his hand into a claw, and he let out a guttural roar. Karen screamed like the little girl she was; while the rest of us laughed till it hurt.

He may have carried it a bit too far one Halloween, though. The trick-or-treaters had thinned out to a slow trickle when Dad decided to sit on the front porch to give out the last of the candy. He placed a bedspread over himself and sat motionless as he tried to assume the shape of the chair in which he sat. He must have done a good job at it because the little one dressed in a cute bunny costume didn't notice anything out of the ordinary. As the unsuspecting youngster reached for the doorbell, Dad stood up and let go that guttural roar again. The pink bunny froze in her tracks and made a puddle on the porch. Her mom, who had waited in the driveway wasn't too pleased.

Like all of us though, Dad had some quirks. My least favorite was his routine of coming home after being on his feet all day, sitting down in the throne, elevating his feet, and calling me over to take his shoes and socks off. They were warm, wet, and smelled to high heaven. Where'd that phrase come from? Heaven probably smells pretty good unless they let Dad take his shoes off! Now that he's gone, I'd give anything to take his shoes off again.

Another quirky habit I didn't care much for was when he'd say, out of the blue; "Come over here, hug my neck, and call me darling. "I guess I always had a sense as to appropriate behavior between two manly men. Once, when visiting my maternal grandfather (the pastor turned street car driver, in Atlanta; he asked me to "give him some sugar." Southerners know what this means and it has nothing to do with sweetening his iced tea. I responded, "Mens don't kiss mens." When it's my time to go home for good and forever; it will be to a trumpet blast; not Dad's whistle, (I believe the Rapture will occur before my death) but either way, Dad will be there like he was for every significant milestone in my life.

Dad's parents; Mama and Papa Jones retired to a small house near Carryville, Florida, in the panhandle about six hours from Jacksonville. They had a large field beside their house where they grew much of their food. Next door; Obie, (Papa Jones' nephew), also grew food. In addition, he had a few cows and a ginormous hog named, Sarah. Obie's mother lived across the road and raised chickens. Obie's Mother, known to all as Aunt Anis was a rather large woman who visited Aunt Gladys (as Mama Jones was known by most family in Carryville.) to use her restroom. My grandparents had the only indoor plumbing for miles. Due to her heft, Aunt Anis frequently broke the toilet seat which aggravated Mama Jones to no end.

Visiting Obie and his wife, Ruth, was like going back in time. With no indoor plumbing, each bed had a large coffee can underneath it for nocturnal necessities. During the day you either went to visit Aunt Gladys or across the road behind Sarah's pen. The back porch had a water pump with a Mayonnaise jar. After pumping the required amount of water, you *always* filled the mayonnaise jar to prime the pump on its next use. I enjoyed visiting Carryville despite the long ride to get there. Third-cousin, Eddie (Obie and Ruth's son) and I fished with cane poles using snored- up worms.

Never heard of those? Snoring up worms entails

driving a short 2x4 stake into the ground and then rubbing the side of an axe head on it. The sound generated sounds like snoring and the vibration irritates the worms causing them to surface. Then you walk around and pick them up off the ground. It was a very long walk to the small gas station/convenience store, but they sold Black Cat fire crackers so we made the effort for the chance to blow stuff up. Our folks turned us loose in the woods with shotguns to go squirrel hunting with no adult supervision; a practice which continued even after I shot Rick in the head.

Relax. I shot him with my BB gun. He was bending over, setting up targets for Eddie and me to shoot. I was aiming at his butt and missed. I blame the incident on Rick. He should never have presented such an irresistible target to a kid brother with a BB gun. Why Eddie didn't shoot too, I'll never know. When third cousin, Eddie married first cousin Candee; their son became my second *and* fourth cousin. (Isn't that how it works?)

We cousins were fairly close in age. The eldest children matched up as did the youngest. This was why Nita and I became close as kids and remain close today. We are close in age, she is a believer, and we have fun taking verbal jabs at each other. With my brain damage, it's a fair battle of wits, now. She is a great encourager. After talking to her on the phone, I always feel uplifted.

With everyone in Carryville growing and sharing their food; a grocery store was not needed. How often do your hear something like this at the breakfast table, today? Mmmm; this sausage is good, is it Sarah? Yes, and we have plenty more of her in the freezer. Slaughter time for Sarah or one of Obie's cows was a community (=

family) event. It seemed Sarah sensed what was going on and she wasn't thrilled about the idea. It took several men to convince her to cooperate and she just plain scared me, so I stayed out of the way.

Mama and Papa Jones had a piano in their small white house with white wagon wheels marking each side of their grass drive way. I loved it when Mama Jones played the piano with gusto while Dad, Karen, and she sang old gospel classics like: *The Old Rugged Cross* and *How Great Thow Art*. Karen sang alto in her school choirs and easily harmonized with Dad and his mother. Dad could sing just about any part. They were good.

Mama Jones was a smoker. Her preferred brand of cigarette came with S&H green stamps which she collected presumably to exchange for merchandise in the S&H catalog. She collected them for years and we'd help count them. We'd joke; Mama Jones, a few more packs of cigarettes and you'll have enough green stamps for your coffin. Smoking eventually contributed to her death in the fall of 1979. The Jones, Dooley, Majors, and Tucker families lost a faithful matriarch that day and we miss her dearly. We miss her greeting in the morning as she stretched away the night's aches, "Mornin' Glory." We lost Papa Jones to cancer in 1965. They've gone on to paradise with Dad to wait for the rest of us for what will be the best family re-union ever! Ready for another joke you can tell your mom? Here you go:

Why is there a strict limit to the number of doors on a chicken coup in some states? – Because if it has four doors, it's a sedan.

CHAPTER IV
BELLA NAPOLI

The Jacobs were the first to leave Joffre Drive. They moved to Virginia for a few years and then returned to Fouraker Road in Normandy village.

Dad aboard the USS Intrepid, 1967

The Joneses tarried a while. Dad took a few more cruises and spent a year at an airbase in South Vietnam. Rick graduated from Paxon High School and earned a Navy ROTC scholarship to the University of South Carolina where he met and married his wife, Sue. Karen completed Jr. High School at Stilwell. I followed in her footsteps later. She then attended the brand- spanking new Ed White High School where she was a member of its first graduating class. All the Jacobs kids are Ed White graduates. Karen decided she didn't see enough of Naples after her birth there in 1955, (*oops*; did I just accidentally reveal my sister's age? – my bad) Karen's specific age isn't important now; for the test later, just remember she's older than me (You *have* been taking notes, haven't you?). With Rick sequestered away at college, Karen came with Dad, Mom, & me when we left in the summer of 1973, shortly after her graduation from Ed White. While in Naples, she was accepted to the University of Maryland, Munich Campus, leaving me alone to take care of our aging parents (mid-40s) and her extra small Chihuahua, Tina, in a foreign country. The flight from Jacksonville to Atlanta was my first time flying. Continuing on to Rome was my first time crossing an ocean, but it wouldn't be my last.

20+ years later, I flew across the same ocean, solo, nonstop, in a plane with only one chair. That's why I was solo. And I did it in less time than Charles Lindberg. But I didn't land in Paris; I landed at RAF Lakenheath in the UK. This is probably why I didn't get a ticker-tape parade like Lucky Lindy.

Bella (Italian for beautiful) wasn't the first adjective to spring to mind when we arrived at Capodichino Airport and drove to our sponsor's home. Napoli (Naples) is a sprawling, crowded, dirty city that takes getting used to. Despite this, the downtown area is filled with piazze (Squares or traffic circles) – Many with fountains, statues, or both. You're never far from a ristarante or pizzeria. The pizza in Naples is without question, the best pizza in the world. It tastes nothing like anything you've had here in the states. You should go there and try it. After you keep reading!

Sometimes snow-capped; sometimes smoking, Mount Vesuvio (Vesuvius), which destroyed Pompeii, Herculaneum and other communities when it erupted in 79AD, sits majestically on the south side of the bay.

Bay of Naples as viewed from FSHS

The resort Isle of Capri sits west of the bay. Every Memorial Day weekend, my family and two others with daughters my age (Layne Gray and Irene Shields) went to Capri. Cherries were in season then so the teens bought a large bag full and ate them all weekend.

Mom & Dad at Capri, 1975

We swam in the clear water at the Marina Grande and visited the Grotta Azzura (Blue Cave); whose entrance was so small visitors laid back in the boat and helped pull it inside via a chain suspended from the entrance ceiling. Once inside, the boat tenders couldn't help but serenade their passengers. The acoustics in the cave coupled with multiple Caruso-wannabees trying to outdo each other made for a lot of sound over the beautiful luminescent blue.

The traffic in Naples is remarkable. Traffic lights and signs were merely suggestions. And if four Fiats abreast fit then lane markings didn't apply. If you hesitate in a piazza (traffic circle); you may never get out of there. Vespa scooters and every other type of motorized two-wheeled vehicles, some with whole families aboard darted everywhere, including the sidewalks.

We stayed with our sponsors (Gerry and Elsie Paul); long enough for our jet lag to wane.

Then Dad learned of a couple planning to travel extensively and needed apartment-sitters during their absence. We fit the bill so we moved in. The apartment was on Via Manzoni atop the Posilipo; the name of the ridge that overlooks the bay from the north. Forrest Sherman High School (FSHS), the school I would soon attend was also on Via Manzoni.

Karen learned that a Baptist church met in FSHS. The next Sunday we attended the church pastored by Ronald MacDonald (no-kidding)! He was Robin's Dad. We called him, Pastor Mac. The Hamburgler was a deacon.

This was a bare-bones operation. The church had no building, organ, piano, or choir robes. Does anyone remember if it had a choir? The Baptismal was five pieces of sheet metal welded together and painted battleship gray. It didn't leak but sitting down on the floor made it awkward for the dunkees to get back to their feet.

At that visit we learned the youth were leaving for summer camp the next day. Karen and I decided to join them. We loaded our stuff onto one of two VW microbuses, piloted by Wally and Teri Otto (the youth pastor and his wife and drove to the church camp; in the foothills northwest of Naples, near the small town of Capua.

The main building was a 400 year-old mill with a large kitchen and enough room for camper gatherings like dining, worship and bible study meetings, or just hanging out. An ice-cold creek fell into a spillway just outside the main building to power the waterwheel driven millstone below. The girls' dorm was in the main building, while the guys had a separate building for our dorm. To swim, we closed the spillway gates and soon an ice-cold pond appeared in which to turn blue. We also had an area suitable for volleyball, close-quarter soccer, and the challenge games Wally and Teri thought up for us. An old monastery on top of one of the nearby hills was a popular destination for climbers. The monastery had a life-size (death-size?) crucifix on the wall. When viewed from the side I got a real sense of Jesus hanging up there and the incredible amount of suffering crucifixion caused its victims. I was humbled to realize the extent of the suffering He *voluntarily* endured for us all.

I loved that old camp and returned every chance I could. That teenage group of strangers was the goofiest group of kids I ever met.

Charlie Lewis was a young sailor stationed at NSA (Naval Support Activity) Naples. He was from Texas and seriously tall; six feet, six inches or two meters if you're into the metric thing. Two-meter Charlie attended our church and helped out with the youth group. Ever try to play ping pong against a 6'6" Texan with arms long enough to return his own serves? Charlie played the guitar and led our singing. My favorite song was a rambling tune Charlie wrote about Moses leading the Israelites across the Red Sea to escape Pharaoh's chariots. When the water fell back in on Pharaoh's army, after the line, "The Egyptians all took a bath," Charlie smiled, dryly and continued," Dirty Egyptians!" In the process of working with us, Charlie and Pastor Mac's daughter,

Robin, became a couple. Nibor (Robin spelled backwards) was just over five feet tall; a foot and a half shorter than Charlie. They later married and moved to North Texas where Charlie became a police officer. Charlie played a fine guitar; but the most impressed I was with him was the day I spotted him sitting in his Fiat, in the NSA parking lot. He was studying his bible - walking the walk. He made a big impact on a teenager that day.

After church camp, my family stayed in one more temporary location before we finally moved into our own home near the beach north of Naples in an area called Ischitella Sud. We lived in a nice place on Viale deghli Oliandri (Oleandre Street) and got on with daily life in Italy. When school started and I officially became a sophomore at FSHS up on via Manzoni. For seat placement in the band, the director went down the line of trumpet players and we played the FSHS fight song. It was as easy as it was cheesy and I was assigned first chair. The section was rounded out with Mike Ward, Jim Steele, and Robin Gillespie, the first female trumpet player I ever met. She was a cutie, so later; I took her to the Prom.

Thus began my high school band geek days. I scored a locker right outside the band room door and keep it for three years. (More grace!)

Our home was located a short walk from the beach. It was also a short walk to my bus stop on the Domiziana, the secondary highway between Pozzuoli (a coastal town north of Naples) and Rome.

La Domiziana is the modern day Appian Way. You could still find paving stones from the original Roman road near The Domiziana. Pozzuoli is mentioned in the

Bible. The New Testament book of Acts (28:13) records Paul's journey to Rome after his arrest. He appealed his case to Caesar as was his right as a Roman citizen. The Bible uses Pozzuoli's Greek name, Puteoli (The New Testament was written in Greek. The Old Testament was written mostly in Hebrew with some Aramaic.

Sometime in 1974, another American family joined our little neighborhood. The Freese Family lived two blocks away. They were also a Navy Family. Mr. Freese worked at Capodichino, so he carpooled with Dad. Mike and Betty Freese are Ohio natives with three children; the oldest, Mike, was a year behind me in school. Child number two, Teresa, was two years behind me. That put all three of us in FSHS at the same time. The third Freese offspring was 12 year-old, Mark, the typical wannabe involved in everything kid brother type. Every week-day morning, I joined Mike and Teresa when they passed our house for the short walk to the Domiziana to wait for Bus One and the forty-minute ride to school.

Mike and I became good friends. We were skiing, sailing, and skim boarding buddies. We won second place in the Naples Naval Sailing Association's inaugural ice-breaker regatta. Mike was the perfect crewman. He was tall, lean and could knock out fifty sit-ups in no time. This combination meant he could hike out on the high side of our fourteen-foot race boat and keep us at just the right amount of heel (lean).

Life was pretty great living in Italy as a teenager, especially during the spring of my senior year when I had my driver's license. Mike and I skied Rocarasso on

Saturday and sailed Pozzuoli Bay on Sunday. It doesn't get much better than that!

Our family travelled quite a bit, too. A good thing about the DOD overseas dependent school system was that missing school to travel with the family was an excused absence. Rome was less than seventy five miles away so we became very familiar with the eternal city. Saint Peter's Basilica is breath-taking and huge. It has markers in the floor to indicate how the other great cathedrals in the world measure up.

My favorite object in the basilica, sits on the right side after you enter. Michelangelo's La Pietà, his masterpiece depicting the crucified Christ lying across Mary's lap. His wounds are there for all to see; another reminder to me of his tortured, excruciating, and let me emphasize, *voluntary* sacrifice. I saw most of Michelangelo's great works. Besides La Pieta, the sculpture that amazed me most was not by Michelangelo.

It sat in a small chapel on a back street in downtown Naples. A 3x5 card tacked to its massive wooden door identified the chapel as La Cappella San Severo.

Inside sat the" Veiled Christ." This piece showed the expired Christ lying on a bed with a sheer veil draped over his body. Beside him laid the crown of thorns, a pair of pliers, a hammer, and three large nails. The bed was trimmed with tassels dangling all around it. The sculpture looked exactly as it was named! It was unbelievable! How do you take hammer and chisel to a piece of marble and make it look like you're looking through a sheer veil, trimmed with lace, draped over a wounded human body? You saw Christ's eyebrows, eyelashes, and beard through the veil. I invite you to Google the places and masterpieces I'm talking about, but mind you, the photos on line don't do them justice.

One of my favorite Italian cities is Firenze. (Florence) It seems those wacky Italians have a different word for everything!

On one of my many visits, I was standing in line to see Michelangelo's David when I realized I had stepped in between a man and his family. When I turned to apologize, I discovered I had cut off Woody Harrelson.

Life *was* way cool living in Italy as a teenager. What did I do to deserve this? Absolutely Nothing! – That's what makes it God's grace.

My favorite day of the week in high school was Tuesday. After school, the youth group piled into the VW Microbuses and went to Wally and Teri's home near Pozzuoli. We called their place "the villa," Once there; we spent the afternoon having fun. We played cards, board games, or Ping-Pong inside. In the driveway, we played basketball. Some even did homework. We enjoyed hanging out with each other. Teri cooked dinner for the group and then after singing *Dirty Egyptians* and other favorites, Wally led a Bible study. Finally, we squeezed back in the VWs for Wally and Teri to deliver us home. Church at FSHS, the villa, and the church camp at the old mill account for most of my fondest memories of my high school years. Several friends came to faith in Christ through Wally & Teri's ministry.

The Freese home was atypical for Italy. It had a garage beneath the first floor with an adjoining room. Mike and I used that room for projects. First, we built a weight bench for buffing up. Next, we built ski racks for the family vehicles. Finally, we built two skim boards. We gave them fancy paint jobs and sealed them with several coats of varnish. They were works of art.

For the unfamiliar, a skim board is a thin, round or bullet shaped board used for skimming - a sport requiring great skill, cunning, and courage- definitely not for the faint of heart. It sometimes scared me and I'm fearless. (a phrase Dad often used)

To skim, the rider waits patiently for a wave to deposit itself and spread out on a flat section of beach. The Bible says, God tells the waves how far they can go. (Job 38:11) So He plays an important role in skim boarding. Once a wave cooperates, the rider takes his board in his hands and sprints onto the expanse of extremely shallow water. Once he achieves maximum velocity, (enough to hurt if he messes up this next step.)The rider then drops the board flat and oh so carefully mounts it with both feet *while maintaining his forward momentum*. (This part is critical.)

I love the Italian people and certainly don't want to stereotype them, but the Naploitani had this one little quirk.

Whenever presented with something out of the ordinary; like skim boarders or an especially small Chihuahuas, the Italians that frequented Lido Ischitella tended to stop and observe. First one; then several, and before you know it, you have a crowd. That always seemed the case when Mike and I took our skim boards to the beach. Lido Ischitella was a popular warm weather Sunday afternoon destination for the Napolitani. So after church up on via Manzoni, we joined the 250,000 Fiats on La Domiziana (four abreast at times) for the long ride home. The empty field across the street from our house became a parking lot. When Mike and I performed for the crowd, some young stallion always emerged wanting to give it a try. Neither Mike nor I knew enough of the language to explain the intricacies of mounting the board like I've done here. Anyone know the Italian word for momentum? These young studs had seen enough to give it a try. So we shrugged, said, "Okay,"(Understood world-wide) and handed them our boards. The young, tanned, hairy, skimmer-wannabe took-off running, dropped the board, and jumped on with both feet, not considering that momentum thing we failed to communicate to them.

The result – The board shot forward at tremendous velocity posing a threat to anyone standing in or near the surf while the Speedo-clad would-be rider lay flat on his back, stunned. This delighted our audience which roared with laughter. "Grazie mille!" (A thousand thanks) The next show starts after we find the skim board." Dove il skim board?

When we travelled, we usually did so with other families: the Freesees and/or the Grays; (Bob, Toni, Layne, and Donna) and/or the Shields; (George, Claire, and Irene.) Bob Gray and George Shields were in Dad's Capodichino carpool.

Layne and Irene were best friends, my age, and attended FSHS. They were also my ski instructors. Our families went to Rocarasso; a small ski resort about two and a half hours from Ischitella. Skiing there was great fun and very inexpensive. To a guy who didn't see snow until after he turned thirteen, and the only mountain he had ever seen was Stone Mountain in Georgia; Rocarasso was a special place. On our first trip there, I had no ski clothes, so I sprayed half a can of Scotch-Guard water repellant on my jeans.

I hauled my rented ski equipment to the slope, d mounted up, and stood there trying to look like I knew what I was doing while Layne and Irene, who had done this before, pushed off and said, "Come on!" I pushed off in hot pursuit and promptly fell down. Gravity strikes again! I guess I needed a little more instruction than, "Come on."

My instructors then explained the basic snowplow technique so I wouldn't die on my first day.

I survived that initial trip to Rocarasso and became immediately hooked on the sport. I bought a subscription to Ski magazine and devoured every word. I also saved my Lira (Italian currency) and took my bargaining skills to an area in downtown Naples known as Thieves' Alley.

In this part of the city, you could find about anything for sale, cheap. It was "Gray Market" merchandise, some still in its original packaging. Apparently, it fell of the truck. Urban Legend said when you were robbed; you could go down to Thieves' Alley and buy your stuff back, cheap. When I had enough with which to bargain, I headed downtown and returned with bright orange Rossignol Stratoflex skis, Solomon bindings, and San Marco boots. No more rentals for me. I was set. Mike made a run to downtown, too. Now we were good to go and we began to get serious about learning to ski with style. (No more snowplow for us) We progressed to skiing with skis parallel and boots so close they touched with no more instruction than Ski Magazine articles, we fell a lot but eventually we got there. No more bunny slopes – Bring on the moguls (bumps) and the deep powder! Another trip to downtown Naples and we emerged with genuine color-coordinated ski apparel. (No more Scotch Guard) Where are they now?

The Grays retired in Arizona and the Shields retired in California. We lost Claire Shields last month. Both my ski instructors joined the Navy. Layne served her career as a cryptologist and married one. They retired in Maine and spend their time either dealing with or running from snow.

Irene worked as a yeoman and became the first woman assigned to an aircraft carrier as the Captain's writer aboard the USS Lexington, a training ship. While aboard the Lexington; Irene met and married a man with whom she had two children. Also aboard the Lexington, a debilitating condition manifest itself which led to Irene's medical retirement from the Navy and in 1998, we lost Irene. She was a fun friend, lousy ski instructor but a talented artist whose works are displayed in my mother's home. The Freeses retired back to Ohio. Mike, a Merchant Marine Academy graduate, is a doctor. Teresa is a grandmother.

On an earlier trip, north, the Shields discovered a slice of heaven; in the Brenner Pass of Austria, the tiny hamlet of Obernberg. Obernberg had only a few buildings straddling a small road and stream running through Alpine pasture land. The road ended at a small lake which fed the stream running down through the valley.

The Gasthaus at Obernberg

The Gasthaus (guest house) was owned and operated by the Meir family —an elderly couple with three sons; Ferdinand, Peter, and Tony. Between them they spoke German, English, and Italian, so communication was never a problem. Obernberg was at high enough elevation that lack of snow was rarely a problem. We stopped for a quick visit one June while driving back to Naples from Munich after picking Karen up for her summer break. It snowed about six inches.

Dad, Mom, & me in Obernberg, June 1975

We became quite enamored with Obernberg and returned often.

My favorite visit was while the '76 Winter Olympics were going on in Innsbruck. We spent two weeks skiing daily either on the hill across the street (The Gasthaus had its own rope tow.) or down the road where a high-speed, quad chairlift waited to take us way up the mountain which took over 45 minutes to descend. This area of the Austrian Alps is known as Tirol. Bavaria (southern Germany) and Tirol are some of my favorite places on earth. Any time of year, the Alps impress. On that two-week trip to Obernberg, the frigid fun continued after the sun went down. At night, Mike, Teresa and I used the ski slope across the road for sledding. Sledding in the dark was a hoot. One evening, our parents left to visit a tavern down the road near the chairlift. We declined their offer to join them to continue night sledding. When our folks returned, they reported the US Ski Team had been at the tavern. I couldn't believe it! I missed them. Through my study of Ski Magazine every month, I was very familiar with the members of the '76 US Ski Team. An even bigger surprise on that trip was my parents taking ski lessons. They were in their mid-forties and risked their old bones on skis. They didn't stay on the hill across the street the whole time. Mom joined me on the high-speed quad! Then she skied all the way back down (The only option.) I was so proud of her! She never took to sailing, though. Like Shirley, She went, but she didn't like it. You could always tell when Dad was heeling the boat too much. The excess heel alarm sounded, "Richard!"

Many years earlier, Dad told my brother and me; if

either of us went to the Naval Academy, he'd buy us a new car when we graduated. He figured buying a car was cheaper than paying for a college education. The Service Academies (USAFA, USNA, and USMA) cost nothing to their appointees. On the contrary, Cadets and Midshipmen draw a small monthly salary since they are on active duty. But after deductions for taxes, uniforms, books, and such, there was barely enough left to cover my phone bill.

Dad had a thing for cars. I already mentioned the green convertible that changed his life plan. Then later, in Jacksonville, he and Mom went shoe shopping and came home with a red, 1964 ½ Ford Mustang. It was a sweet ride but with a family of five; all three kids were relegated to the small back seat. As the youngest, I volunteered to sit on the hump. Uncomfortable – yes. But that didn't stop us from driving it to Atlanta to show it off. I saw snow for the first time on that trip up north.

Dad's greatest automotive acquisition came toward the end of our time in Naples.

In the seventies; gas prices skyrocketed in Europe. As a result, many Italians sold their extra or fuel inefficient cars. Dad somehow connected with a man who sold him a 1964 Mercedes- Benz 230SL for around $1,500US. The SL was a two-seat roadster with a removable hardtop and a cloth top which folded and hid away in a compartment between the trunk and backseat, for a very clean look with the hardtop off and the ragtop stowed away. The car needed a little cosmetic work but it ran great and fast. Dad had the interior re-done and gave it a fresh paint job.

Prom date, Robin Gillespie and me, 1976

Dad's car incentive program worked on me and since I only knew Navy, I figured I'd try for Annapolis and the car deal with no intent on continuing with the plan Lindy and I devised earlier. I had already blown the remaining faithful part of the deal and was infatuated with a cheerleader in the youth group who agreed to write after we left for college. Then there was the pen pal from the Stilwell Band that needed to be checked out once I returned to the States. Sorry, Lindy, the deal's off.

I suspected it would take more than good grades, solid SAT scores, and band to secure the required congressional appointment. I needed to play on one of my school's athletic teams- but which one?

I had never played organized sports growing up in Jax. I was one of the better athletes in Normandy Village but all we played was sandlot baseball, touch football, and our version of kill the man with the ball. I needed to learn the game of football and get some experience before I talked to Coach Dayton. My solution was to play in the Pop Warner League.

As a high- school student, I was older than most in the league; but at five feet, four inches tall and one-hundred and thirty pounds, I made the Wolverine Roster as an offensive lineman.

We played at Carney Park, an extinct volcano crater with a US Forces recreational area in it. Carney Park had the only American football and baseball fields in the region, a nine-hole golf course, a pool, cabins for overnighting, a snack bar, and a small drive-in theater.

Prior to one of our football games, our punter warmed up. I caught his punts and threw the ball back for another kick. After several catches, Coach Castro; seeing I could catch, made me the punt return man for the game starting in a few minutes. Eventually, our defense prevailed and the other team was forced to punt. I took my position to receive the punt.

The kick was long forcing me back up to catch it. In the process, the ball slipped through my hands and bounced between my legs continuing several yards behind me. How am I doing so far? I turned around, ran back to the ball, picked it up, tucked it away, and ran. (*Run, Forrest, run!*) I went left first and saw the coming hordes shift left, too. Then I cut back to the right behind some blockers. The hordes didn't match this move so it was off to the races. I continued right and then sprinted up the sideline and scored after a seventy-five yard return. We eventually won the game. Coach Castro moved me to running back and sent me home with the playbook.

During the next game, I scored on my first play from

scrimmage. The whole inexplicable season continued like this. (Grace? – you bet!) I set league records in nearly every rushing category; the one I remember to this day over forty years later, was my 14.7 average yards per carry. Word got back to Coach Dayton and he asked me to join the FSHS Football team. I was delighted to. Although my size kept me from playing near as much as I did in Pop Warner.

My quest to get on the FSHS football team roster worked. My extracurricular activities plus solid academic performance (All God-given talents) won me an appointment to USAFA from Florida congressman, the honorable Charles Bennett. Why not Annapolis? Clearly, *God wanted me in the Air Force.* I later learned that congressmen have a limited number of slots allocated to them for appointments to each of the service Academies. Congressman Bennett only had a slot to USAFA to offer me. Now all I needed was for USAFA to accept me.

FSHS 1976 football team, I'm number 20

I'm convinced that had the Navy not moved us overseas when it did, my life would have turned out very differently.

Had I gotten my way and followed my band friends to Ed White, I would have been lost in a class of over six hundred, instead of the 101 in the class of '76 at FSHS. And I wouldn't have experienced teenage life in Europe or the extraordinary things you'll read about soon.

One afternoon, in late April of my senior year, Dad came home from work with our mail and I could tell something was up by his body language. Mom, Dad, and I sat on the sofa (hint #1). Dad handed me an envelope with a USAFA return address (hint#2). The letter inside was dated April 15, 1976 and signed by an Air Force Lieutenant General. The USAFA Superintendent was welcoming me to the class of 1980! I was to report to the Academy on June 28th. (No more hints, *I'm in!*). Now we're talking! Mom and Dad watched for my reaction.

I said, "Well, I guess I'll be a pilot." It was the first time I seriously considered flying as a career. To be honest, I was surprised I got in. Then it dawned on me that I was going to Colorado and the Rocky Mountains. I was headed for ski country, USA for four years! Want to get a kid who grew up in Florida excited? Show him mountains and show him snow, two things found only in Disney World in Florida.

On a recent trip to Florence; I had drooled over a pair of top-of-the-line Rossignol skis in the window of a sports store. The youth group later made a trip to Florence where we toured the city and spent the night in a youth hostel before returning home the next day. I had saved $500US from a youth-hire program the previous summer.

I worked in the Supply Department at Capodichino joining Dad's carpool. I had plenty of money to buy the Rossignol ST Comps. With the money I had left over I went to Thieves' Alley and bought Solomon bindings (top-shelf equipment) and a pair of high-end San Marco boots. *Now* I was ready for USAFA. Or so I thought.

Before I left Italy, my parents hosted a cookout in our backyard. The usual suspects were there (Grays, Shields, and Freeses) plus my girlfriend, Robin Gillespie. (Trumpet playing prom date).

Toward the end of the festivities, Dad made a short speech, lifted a dinner plate, and smashed it to pieces with a hammer. This symbolized I was going to be on my own now. I was to fend for myself. Looking back; I think this was genius and I plan to do the same with my son, if I should have one.

At the airport; Dad put his arm around me and said, "Remember, son, no matter how tough it gets out there in Colorado, you can't come back here!" With that heart-touching sendoff, I picked up my one small suitcase, my ski gear, and got in line. The flight from Naples to Rome was brief. Continuing on from Rome to Atlanta was a tad (Southern for a little bit) longer.

I flew into Atlanta to see relatives. I stayed with Aunt Voncile who lived near Stone Mountain. Mama Jones lived in her basement, which was finished off nicely for that purpose. I didn't stay around Atlanta long because I borrowed Karen's Ford Falcon (which Mama Jones was keeping) and drove to Pensacola to visit Rick and his family. Then I drove to Jax to catch up with old friends. I stayed with my future in-laws. While out on a date one evening with a former clarinet-playing cutie from Stilwell (the pen pal), I noticed the Falcon needed gas.

No problem, I pulled into a gas station, parked beside the pump, and waited." What are you doing?" Pam asked. "We need gas." I answered. "Why are you just sitting here?" she asked. I told her I was waiting for the attendant to come out and fill us up. She giggled and said, "We don't do that anymore; it's all self-serve now." Geez, how long was I gone? "Can you show me how?" That's right; a girl had to teach me how to pump gas! –Lame. After several days courting Miss Lewellyn from my future in-laws' house in my sister's car; it was time to drive back to Atlanta and get this Air Force college thing going. As the fateful date of 28 Jun '76 approached, I must admit I was getting nervous. I had breakfast with Mama Jones in her kitchen every morning and marveled at how much Dad looked like her. Sixteen year-old cousin, Nita, drove me around in her new Jeep (She was a spoiled child.) Everywhere we went; I saw a car model I didn't recognize and asked Nita what it was. That's right, I had to learn about the seventies muscle cars from my girl cousin! – Lame again.

Eventually, the calendar compelled me to continue my journey west to Colorado Springs.

After deplaning, I collected my few belongings and proceeded outside into the bright Colorado sun. The first thing I couldn't help but notice was the rampart range just to the west; chief among them is Pike's Peak at 14,110 feet. Outside the airport sat a fleet of USAFA buses.

I selected one, placed my suitcase and ski equipment in the baggage compartment, and climbed aboard. Like everyone else, there must have been a trace of trepidation on my face. Sporting our jeans and long '70s hair; we sized each other up. (Was I as good as he was in high school?) Then I noticed there were a few girls. Girls?! Here?! It turned out the class of 1980 was the first class with women.

I mostly stared out the window on the ride from the airport up to USAFA's Cadet Area. This place was very different from my native Florida. And there wasn't a Fiat to be seen. We pulled into a parking lot at the base of the "Bring Me Men" Ramp. This politically incorrect ramp was wide enough for a squadron of one hundred cadets to march from the terrazzo-level of the Cadet Area down to the parade field. The name came from a line in a line in a Horace Greely poem: Bring me men to match my mountain… When instructed to do so; we got off the bus and took position on a set of yellow foot prints which were painted on the pavement. So, there we stood; busloads of disoriented eighteen year-olds standing in perfect rank and file, thanks to the painted footprints. Eventually, a cadet introduced himself, and began calling names from a roster. Can you believe some people didn't show up?

Did they just change their minds? Or maybe they missed their flight. Was this a culling process? If you didn't have the brains and motivation to make it from your hometown to these painted-on footprints; maybe you weren't cut out for the Air Force. I made it, and I came from Europe. Do I get bonus points for that? – Nope.

By the end of the first day, we were assigned to our Basic Cadet Training (BCT) units, sworn in, issued uniforms, had our hair cut off, and assigned a room in Vandenberg Hall, a six-story,1/4 mile-long dormitory on the north side of the terrazzo.

CHAPTER V
USAFA

The USAF Academy (USAFA); pronounced You-Sof'-Uh is enormous (18,500 acres).

USAFA

The puny little service academies at West Point and Annapolis would probably fit on our Intramural fields. USAFA is also high at 7258 feet.

Pushed up against Colorado's Rampart range, north of Colorado Springs; the campus is also isolated, as opposed to USNA which sits in the middle of a city. The middies can see and hear civilization. They can walk out the gate to numerous restaurants, clubs, shops, and the city docks. I've never been to West Point but was told it looks like a prison. At USAFA, its nine miles to the south gate and several miles further on Academy Blvd or I-25 to Colorado Springs.

The newest of the service academies (construction was completed in 1954); USAFA has a modern look. The two dormitories have aluminum–framed glass exteriors as does Harman Hall; where the Superintendent and Commandant of Cadets have their offices. We liked to say USNA and USMA have 200 years of tradition unhampered by progress. The academic building, the social center, and the massive dining hall, Mitchell Hall or Mitch's (all four thousand cadets eat together in about twenty minutes.) add marble siding to their architecture.

The striking Cadet Chapel and a few other buildings round out the modern look to the cadet area. They hem in the terrazzo which is a large paved area in the middle of the cadet area at the third floor level. It is paved with small aggregate stones and partitioned by marble strips.

The terrazzo

A large grassy area with a small hill (Spirit Hill) occupies the middle of the terrazzo. Aircraft sit in the four corners of the grassy area. Two of them, an F-4 and F-105 are Vietnam War memorials and not to be touched. The other two, a T-38 and an F-104 were fair game, although I never heard of the T-38 being messed with. The F-104; on the other hand, was pushed around on the terrazzo for years. The most popular destination for the old Starfighter was in front of the doors to Mitchell Hall in the hope that the obstruction would not be cleared in time for the cadet wing to march to the next meal. I don't think this ever happened.

Basic Cadet Training (BCT) or "beast" began on those yellow footprints and lasted six weeks. The first three weeks (first beast) was confined to the cadet area. This time exposed the new cadet to life at the Academy as an underclassman. The new cadet was issued a little book, *Contrails*, which contains the USAF history, USAFA's history, USAF organization, USAF, sister service, and foreign military aircraft, and numerous "dead guy quotes" and songs (Do you know how many verses our national anthem has?); This whole book needed to be memorized yesterday; so every free minute, found that little book in front of our faces.

FAVORITE QUOTE:

War is an ugly thing, but not the ugliest of things; the decayed and degraded state of moral and patriotic feeling which thinks nothing is worth a war, is worse. A man who has nothing which he cares more about than he does about his personal safety is a miserable creature who has no chance at being free, unless made and kept so by the exertions of better men than himself. (John Stuart Mills)

MOST IRONIC QUOTE:

The discipline which makes the soldiers of a free country reliable in battle is not to be gained by harsh or tyrannical treatment. On the contrary, such treatment is more likely to destroy than to make an army. (Major General John Schofield's address to the West Point graduating class of 1879.) We frequently recited this quote while field stripping our rifles with upperclassmen shouting words of encouragement in each ear.

In first beast we learned to march, salute, and execute the sixteen-count rifle manual with our demilitarized, heavy, WWII-era M-1 rifles. Our uniform for first beast was typically our light-weight dark blue pants; a short sleeved light blue shirt, with a nametag, black socks, and highly polished, black, low quarter shoes. We wore no insignia or rank because we had done nothing to earn either. We were just Doolies – one of several terms of respect and high regard given USAFA freshman. Others include Smack, Wad, Maggot or just plain Mister.

The flight cap we wore does not cover one's ears. For most of us; our ears had been covered with hair for years before day one of beast. The bright Colorado sun, which is more intense due to the altitude, had its way with our tender, lily-white ears and they burned. We were issued sun block but none of us geniuses thought to use it on our ears.

Indoors, we walked quickly (like you have a purpose, mister!) on the right side of the hall, giving way to everyone who outranked us – which included everyone. Outside, we ran everywhere.

Did I mention the 7258 feet altitude? Ever feel like your lungs were on fire? Run at 7258 feet after being at sea-level since inception!

On the terrazzo, Doolies were required to stay on

the marble strips. So you couldn't run directly anywhere; you had to follow the square corners of the marble strips. Back indoors; you did something similar; you squared all corners as if you were marching. As Doolies, we were always at an exaggerated attention; which was designed to hurt; your head was erect, your chest was out, your shoulders were back and down to the point your shoulder blades nearly touched, and you tucked your chin in as far as it would go creating numerous little chins under your neck; the more – the better. (I want to see chins- more chins, Maggot!) This looked ridiculous. It was hard to not bust out laughing when you saw the contortions a classmate endured when accosted by an upperclassman. But woe to he who scoffs at his classmate! Get in front of a mirror, and try it, and see if you don't laugh. Then try it at the dinner table. Try eating like this with your eyes fixed on the Academy emblem on top of your plate. Looking around was called gazing and not tolerated. Eating this way was not the worst thing about eating at Mitchell's.

Second beast (the last three weeks of BCT) began with a move (read: forced march) to a place named Jack's Valley.

In Jack's Valley, we played army; we slept on cots in tents, we conducted a most our training outside wearing fatigues and combat boots (highly polished, of course). We qualified on the M-16. We ran the Obstacle course causing the lungs to burn again. We negotiated the bayonet assault course where we mounted bayonets on our M-1s and thrust them into stuffed, burlap dummies (shouting "Kill! Kill! Blood makes the grass grow! Kill!" with each thrust) we crawled in the dirt under barbed wire while grenade simulators and small arms fire were going off. You'd have thunk we'd just cleared the beaches at Normandy. But I thought this was the Air Force! Are the dudes at WestPoint flying? What are we doing in the dirt?! It wouldn't be the last time I played Army in my career. I'll play a little Navy, too. Jack's Valley also had the Confidence Course.

This course had obstacles to negotiate requiring you to trust teammates with your life. The scariest was a multi-story tower we loved to climb. To do so, you stood on the edge of the floor (There were no walls), reached up and placed your hands on the floor above and then swung out as you lifted yourself and threw your legs up to the floor above where a teammate waited to grab your legs and assist you complete your ascent. This was no problem until you were ten floors up. Then it became less about confidence building and more about fear suppression. We rounded out our training with land navigation and pugil-stick contests. (Not fun).

With beast behind us, the class of 1980 was ready to join the cadet wing as fully trained doolies where life changed little. We still had to stay on the marble strips but at least we could walk now.

Following beast, we were assigned to one of the forty cadet squadrons in the wing. I was assigned to CS-01(Fun One) along with new friends; Tom Heemstra (Heembo) from Michigan, and Steve Streiffert (Streif) from Alaska. CS-01 was located on the fifth floor of Vandenberg Hall.

Roommates were assigned to us as doolies, and mine were memorable. First, was the sometimes goofy and always difficult to understand, Jeff Roberts from West

Virginia. Jeff struggled with academics and washed out by Christmas. Next was John Cherniga; a vain, soft-spoken guy from Ft. Walton beach, Florida. John asked me to take pictures of his hair from every angle because he had gotten it just right. Granted; It *was* a big deal when our hair grew out long enough to part several months after beast, but a photo spread to show barbers was over the top.

Joe Accardo was an Italian American from New York. He was quite the ladies-man and had an enthusiastic opinion on everything. Joe was a very likeable guy, a good athlete, and a natural leader. Somewhere along the career I heard that Joe was flying F-15s. I wasn't surprised. He probably sought out that career path because *Eagle Drivers get all the hot chicks*. Finally, there was the knucklehead of the class; Jim Crump. Jim had a propensity for staying in trouble for easily avoidable infractions he brought on himself. He'd forget to take his hat off when he came inside or mouth off at an upperclassman.

After a particularly heavy blizzard; the snow had drifted up against the wall beside the Bring Me Men Ramp. Some foolhardy cadets jumped from the terrazzo-level, three stories up into the snow drifts below. The wing staff announced over the PA system for cadets to refrain from this dangerous practice.

That was all the encouragement Crump needed. He proceeded to the top of the ramp and climbed up on the top of the wall to make his leap of faith. Faith that he would miss the fire hydrants at the base of the wall and faith that the fine powdery snow, for which Colorado is famous, would slow his 180-pound self down enough to prevent serious injury if he found one of those hydrants.

The top of the ramp is visible from the wing command post. So, Crump should not have been surprised to find some wing staffers in the vicinity. They ordered Jim to get down from his perch. He turned, attempted to divert their attention by pointing to the sky (with his middle finger) and jumped. One of the wing staffers ran/slid down the ramp after him and Jim Crump was busted. He marched many tours for that slight lapse in judgment.

Jim and I agreed to dislike each other immediately. He told me I was a Mama's boy and I thought he was the smartest moron I ever met.

Years later, I learned Jim got into a lot of trouble as a T-38 Instructor Pilot (IP) at Columbus AFB, MS as a result of poor flight discipline (typical Crump) after his IP assignment; he was assigned to fly the KC-135 Stratotanker, the least desired assignment for aT-38 IP.

Doolies were not allowed to use the elevators in the dorms. Nor could we use the coke machines, TV room, or the foosball table. These were reserved for upper classmen which included everyone but Doolies.

Seniors were called Firsties; juniors were two degrees, and sophomores were three degrees. Only Firsties could own cars and have TVs in their rooms. Only upper classmen could have stereos in their rooms and wear civilian clothes off duty.

Cadet Squadrons are made up of one hundred cadets. We were organized with a cadet squadron commander and operations officer (both Firsties), a cadet first sergeant (a two-degree). The rest of the squadron was divided into four flights led by cadet flight commanders. (Firsties). The flights were made up of elements led by Element sergeants (two-degrees). The adult supervision of the squadron rested with the Air Officer commanding or AOC, an active duty officer from the "real Air Force."

Doolies were housed three to a room furnished with a single bed and a bunk bed. We each had a desk under a wall-mounted bookcase for our textbooks and cadet regulations binder. We shared a sink that remained dry during the day and a trashcan which remained empty. In short, the room remained inspection-ready at all times.

We each also had a dresser for our folded clothes which were folded in accordance with the regs that binder which sat on the bookcase: underwear (4" x 4"), T-shirts (4" x 6"). To make this requirement easier, we cut cardboard to the proper dimensions and wrapped a sacrificial garment around it for the top of the stack. Our socks were rolled up from toe to top and tucked under to create a neat little bundle. Tucking the roll in the top created a "smile" on one side of the bundle. Our top dresser drawer had dividers in them the exact width of a rolled up sock. So our socks were lined up with the smiles oriented the same way. Our closets would make a mother proud, too. Our uniforms were hung neatly on hangers which were evenly spaced; our shiny black shoes and boots were evenly spaced on the shoe rack as were our hats on the closet shelf. Each desk had one florescent lamp on it. The books on the bookcase were sized from tallest (towards the front) to shortest with their spines flush with the edge of the shelf. A rack beside the door held our rifles.

Our beds were made with hospital corners requiring a ruler and a spray water bottle or starch to make them crisp.

There was no bedspread; only a gray blanket over the sheets and mattress pad. This blanket also had hospital corners and was tucked in tight. Many used safety pins to secure the top sheet and blanket to the springs under the bed to keep it pulled tight. Another gray blanket was folded in a prescribed manner so that only folded edges were exposed. It rested at the foot of the bed. Some resorted to sleeping on top of their beds rather than sleeping under the covers to make preparing the bed the following day faster. Our pillows were shoved into their pillow cases sideways and the excess pillowcase was folded over and tucked in tight to make a tight, firm, presentable pillow. This was how we maintained our rooms on a daily basis.

But occasionally, we had formal room inspections on Saturday Mornings called SAMIs. These were white glove inspections conducted by squadron leadership. We worked late into the night on Friday; usually waiting on a floor buffer- (guess who got them last.) For these inspections we waited patiently standing in our rooms for the inspection party to arrive. We didn't sit because it wrinkled our pants. (Our uniform was inspected, too.)

We bored quickly and got creative. A tennis ball usually passed the time nicely with only a slight chance at getting caught. All doors were open while the squadron was inspected room-by-room.

By bouncing the tennis ball off the wall across the hall you made the cadets next door scramble a bit to find and hide it before they were inspected. If the ball returned, you simply sent it back sometimes on fire. The new fuzzy ones plus a squirt of lighter fluid worked best for this.

Pre-inspection pranks to force your victims to work well into the night were often mean.

For example, some lighter fluid applied generously to an unwanted vinyl LP album was lit and slid under the victim's door after they went to bed for the evening. The blaze got their attention so they're wide awake to witness the record melt on their freshly buffed and shiny floor. I said they were mean! I suppose cadets are using unwanted CDs for this practice today. The doors had vents over them so sometimes; we squirted lighter fluid in the vent and it ran down the inside of the door and puddled on the floor. Then we lit it off. It's amazing that place hasn't burned down after all these years!

Another more extreme example required a hose, a condom, and a silk pillowcase. None of which were cadet issue items. The idea was to connect the hose to the faucet in the victim's room and place the other end in the condom, and then place the condom in the pillow case while it rests on the victim's bed. Then turn the water on very slowly. The condom expanded as it filled with water. In fact, it expanded to fill the total volume of the pillow case. Next, ever-so-carefully slide the pillow case out from around the condom (this is why a silk pillow case works best). When the bed's owner returns to find this huge water-filled blob on this bed that he dare not move or even touch for fear of busting it; he'll wish he had paid more attention to room security. There were also stories of cherry bombs taped to a can of Comet to cover the entire room with the fine green powder. Super gluing items on the desktop was easy and fun. In addition to our SAMIs, we also had occasional uniform/rifle inspections called, in ranks inspections (IRIs). These inspections were conducted on the terrazzo while we stood at attention with our rifles at our sides by our sides. We stood in open ranks – the extra space was required for the rifle inspection. When the inspector stopped in front of you, you executed your best move to port arms(holding the rifle in front of your body) followed by inspection arms (hitting the rifle's receiver lever with the side of your extended, rigid, and white-gloved left hand and crisply looking down and back up as if verifying an empty chamber. This took practice to avoid hitting the inspector or breaking your left hand. Sometimes; after an IRI, since the cadet wing was all dressed up and carrying our rifles; we had a parade. Cue music – Off we marched; while the USAFA band played martial tunes at 120 beats per minutes,. down the Bring me Men Ramp, and on down to the parade field. CS-01 was first on the field and we left neat furrows in the grass for the rest of the wing to follow. A tough Saturday was referred to as a triple threat when had a SAMI was followed by an IRI, and parade. Those cadets planning on spending the rest of the day elsewhere couldn't wait to get this nonsense completed.

Time away from the Academy was infrequent. As a dooly we were allowed one weekend pass per semester (you could leave after duty on Friday and return by call-to- quarters (eight p.m.) on Sunday. You also got three off duty privileges (ODPs) per trimester. With an ODP you could leave the Academy after duty on any day and return by call-to-quarters (8 pm).

Let's return to the more annoying aspects of being a freshman at USAFA:

For instance, Doolies were required to say a greeting to every upperclassman they passed which is everyone but a classmate and the insignia that differentiate the classes can be difficult to spot without gazing so we accidentally greeted each other frequently. Another pain-in- the-neck dooly task was calling minutes.

The cadet's day was highly regulated – Wake up to Reveille; march to breakfast, go to class, march to lunch, go to class, play intramural sports, march to dinner, study until lights out at taps(11:00pm), go to bed; repeat for 1461 days.

This schedule is regulated by bugle calls over the P.A. system and backed up by doolies calling minutes. The most important formation of the day is the noon-meal formation. All forty squadrons formed up on the terrazzo and marched one after the other while the USAFA band played. Tourist lined the wall at the Cadet Chapel to watch this spectacle; four thousand people all dressed alike walking to lunch together to the beat of the music. Urban legend had it that USAFA was second only to Disneyland as a tourist destination west of the Mississippi. To ensure everyone made it to formation on time, doolies called minutes.

We positioned ourselves at strategic locations throughout the squadron. Only one of us could see a clock without gazing. Beginning with fifteen minutes until first call (the bugle call played before horse races. (You'd all recognize it.) The doolies shouted *in unison*: Sir, There are fifteen minutes until first call for the noon-meal formation; the uniform is _____. The menu is _____. There are fifteen minutes until first call!

You all better stop at the same time. Then you stood there at attention, waiting do it again each minute until the bugle sounded.

We were extremely vulnerable during this time to having our uniforms and/or haircuts inspected or questioned about just about anything from any upperclassman. What's on the menu for dinner? We memorized the menus for all three meals for the day. For fun(theirs only) some upperclassmen stood uncomfortably close and stared, trying to make you smile or laugh while calling minutes. The discipline quote? No problem, sir. I've got it right here. How about I throw in the third verse of the Air Force song? You want the century-series fighters? Let's see, are those the ones that start with the North American F-100 Super saber, right? Just kidding.

Doolies could only answer with the correct response (recommended); yes sir, No sir, and Sir, I do not know. (Doolies weren't allowed to use contractions.). The answer to a "Why" question was ways No excuse, sir. (Even if you knew why)If they really wanted to know why, they ordered, give me a reason. So a real conversation between a dooly and upperclassman could go something like this:

Mister Jones! Yes sir! Were you just gazing? Sir, I do not know! Why not! No excuse, sir! Give me a reason! Sir, I can't see my eyeballs! You what?! Sir, I *cannot* see my eyeballs.

We ate our meals family-style. (What a dysfunctional family!) Three Firsties sat at the head of the table with two-degrees and three-degrees-degrees filling in the side seats to monitor the three doolies sitting around the end of the table. We were responsible for passing out the food and drink when the waiter brought his food cart to the table. One of us would ask the waiter's name and before left, we would address him loud enough for all to hear, "Thank you Mr.___." If we forgot this, we could expect the following:

Mister Jones! Yes sir! What's the waiter's name? Sir, I do not know! Why not?! No excuse, sir! Give me a reason! Sir, I wasn't paying attention when cadet Accardo asked him! That's weak, Jones. Yes sir! Mister Jones, find out what the waiter's name is. Yes sir. Sir, may I ask a question? (I just did.). Yeah, go ahead. Sir may I address my classmate C4C Crump? No, Jones you can't ask Crump the waiter's name. Sir, my I be excused? Yeah, go ahead. I got up and sped down the row of tables in search of our waiter. I didn't get a good look at him but recognized his voice as Mr. Bruce. The wing suspected he was gay because of is effeminate voice. I soon spotted him (without gazing, mind you.) and my supposition was confirmed when I read his nametag. For a moment, I contemplated going over to the "jock ramps" to eat. The athletes ate together and the doolies were permitted to eat at rest like a normal person. Had I done this. Though, I might have been accosted by one of the upperclassmen at my table for abandoning my classmates and being weak again. So I returned to my seat and was permitted to rejoin the table, provided I knew the waiter's name. (Mr. Bruce)

Mr. Crump, Is that right? Yes sir! Mr. Accardo?! Yes sir! We sat at attention with our eyes fixed on the Air Force seal at the top of our plates to prevent gazing. Our bites had to be small enough to choke down quickly. We were granted five chews to respond if addressed by an upperclassman.

We used the AF Form O-96 to critique every meal. The doolies were responsible for filling out this official Air Force form. It had boxes to check and an area for written comments. I can't remember the six individual services critiqued by checking the boxes, but we always checked the boxes: labeled Fast, Neat, Average, Friendly, Good, Good.

For the write-in section; we were required to remember comments voiced at the table. (Gazing was a crime but eavesdropping was required)

Then we asked the firstie at the head of the table after making sure he wasn't chewing (because it would be uncivilized to interrupt a firstie while he's chewing. (Try that without gazing!) When he was available, we asked, "Cadet Firstie, sir!" "Yeah, go ahead. "Sir, Do you or any other gentlemen at the table have any remarks or suggestions for the form oh dash nine- six?" Then we were bombarded with, several, "yeah, tell them..." I handed over the completed for close scrutiny. "Mister Jones, you checked the friendly box, but we said the waiter was a jerk (This is why his name was so important.). Why? "No excuse, sir. Give me a reason. Sir, because we *always* check the friendly box; and there isn't, pardon me, please, sir, *is not* a Jerk box.

Once the Form 0-96 passed scrutiny, an upperclassman yelled, "Get up!" or "On your feet!" and we sprang to attention behind our chairs waiting for the next command like well-trained German Shepherds. The firstie shouted, "Post!" and the doolies responded in unison, "Excuse me, please, Good Afternoon sir! _____!" The blank was filled in with an appropriate pre -arranged exclamation such as Beat Navy! To which the upperclassmen still left at the table typically responded, "Yeah, beat 'em. Now get outa here!" We then executed flawless facing maneuvers and got outa there. We had just enough time to get back to our rooms, collect books for our afternoon classes and get to class on those cursed marble strips.

The real meal challenge came when the table assignments were messed up and some poor dooly was forced to cruise the 400 tables looking for an empty dooly seat *sans gazing*. Once located, this poor schmuck had to ask permission to join the table, often having to prove himself worthy by satisfactorily answering a barrage of questions.

Then the other doolies at the table began to sweat. We've got to let this guy or gal know what to say for the post! The sharp dooly (like me) had it written on a piece of paper to secretly pass to unexpected guests. It was then up to the guest to discretely read and memorize it. There were several ways to do this on the sly. But the upperclassmen knew the challenge we faced and were extra vigilant for suspicious activity at our end of the table.

If caught, the upperclassmen confiscated the piece of paper, read the post, declared it no good, and tore it up. Gulp. Now I had to come up with another clever post, write it down, and share it with two people who had to read and memorize it without detection. This was madness!

One evening of my dooly year, I thought my cadet days might be numbered few. The class of '80 was assembled in Arnold Hall's auditorium. After the event concluded, all

900+ of us had to get back to our rooms; most of which were in Vandenberg Hall. Almost all of us were headed the same way on the marble strips that were only wide enough for one person. I had injured my ankle and was creating a traffic jam, so I pulled aside to let my classmates pass.

While standing there exposed, a rather large African American upperclassman approached and stood very close to me to be intimidating. It worked. "Okay, smack," who am I? Why, did you forget? Sir, you are Cadet Jackson. (At least that's what his nametag said.) "What's my rank?" Do you know nothing about yourself? Sir, I do not know. "Why not?" No excuse sir. "Give me a reason." Sir, you are standing so close, I cannot see your shouderboards. In fact, he was standing so close, he pressed against the bill of my wheel cap causing it to cover my eyes. He backed up a step and leaned down to allow me to see his shoulder boards, giving me a temporary reprieve from his foul breath. A shower would be a good idea, too. "Well, smack?" Sir, you are Cadet Colonel Jackson. "What's my job?" Harassing injured freshmen in the dark? And you do it quite well, I might add. Sir, I do not know. You don't know your group staff?! I assume from your reaction that I do not, sir. "Well, Cadet Jones, (at least he knows who I am.)Who is your element leader? Sir, my element leader is C1C Baumgartner.

"Report to Cadet Baumgartner tonight and tell him you don't know your group staff." "Make sure you report to him tonight, maggot, because I know Cadet Baumgartner and I'll find out if you don't." Right, there's 4000 of us on this campus and *you* just happen to know *my* element leader. We have an honor code so I had to believe this guy. Yes sir; Good evening sir. Go Away – uh, I mean, Beat Navy! "Yeah, beat 'em."

Great! How am I doin' now? I went straight to my room and asked my roommates, "What's a group staff?" They told me who was on the group staff as I wrote it down and quickly began memorizing it. Why do you guys know this and I don't? We pay attention.

Do you guys know where Baumgartner's room is? I've got to go tell him I'm stupid. Yeah, hang a right just past the showers. His room is down a ways on the left.

It turned out Cadet Colonel Jackson was the commander for first group, the group under which CS-01 fell.

I hobbled off to find my element leader's room to confess my sin. When I sensed I was close to being "down a ways, past the showers" I stopped to execute a facing move to see the nametags by the doors. I wouldn't want to be gazing, would I? I knocked onC1C Baumgartner's door and he indicated that I could enter, which I did.

Sir, cadet fourth class Jones reporting as ordered. "Who ordered you to report to me?" Sir, Cadet Colonel Jackson told me to tell you that I do not know my group staff. He stopped me on the way back from Arnold Hall. "Well, do you know who he is now?" Yes sir. "How about the rest of the group staff?" I am working on it, sir. "Okay, don't worry about it. You can go." Mission accomplished. I limped back to my room and finished memorizing the first group staff in case Cadet Jackson jacked me up on the way to breakfast.

The Dooly year culminated with Hell Week, which

is a bit of a misnomer, because it didn't last seven days. It only felt that way. It began Sunday evening at call-to quarters and ended on Wednesday after the acceptance parade.

The whole point of Hell Week was to punctuate the end of the dooly year and be accepted into the cadet wing as upperclassmen before the next class of freshmen showed up for BCT. Hell Week was scheduled after the semester's classes terminated but before the summer programs began. If we survived, we were presented with our coveted prop and wings insignia to pin on our flight caps. But more importantly, we were called by our first names or nicknames (I was Jonesy) and we didn't have to navigate on marble strips, greet everything that moved, or eat at attention. The training approach was simple. First, break us down (individually and as a group). Give us impossible tasks and push us to the limit; then slowly let us succeed, and see the end in sight, then fire us up and make us feel invincible. Then be done and accept us as one of their own. During the week, most of us lost our voices due to days of shouting.

The upperclassmen continually reminded us Hell Week was approaching. They seemed giddy about the stress and angst they were about to impose. It was all mind games and it worked. We were terrified of Hell Week.

The doolies of CS-01 had a party in a C Springs hotel the Saturday night before Hell Week began as did most doolies in the wing. At the appointed time on Sunday evening, we were directed to stand in open ranks with our rifles in the squadron assembly room (SAR). We happily complied. We had no choice. While standing there, the class of '79, who were responsible for our "training" marched in the room and stood in formation before us at the front of the room. They were staring us down, drooling for dooly meat

The cadet squadron commander then entered and said, "Class of '79, fall out and make corrections." Then we were corrected. The three-degrees rushed in our ranks and raged all over us. We were field stripping rifles while reciting the discipline quote followed by the cargo aircraft followed by anything and everything in *Contrails*. We were doing squat-thrusts, push-ups and all manner of physical exertion for the tiniest mistake.

What a great way to release all that pent-up tension and stress. Thanks,'79! The "training" went on for what seemed like forever. Eventually, it ended about the time we were getting warmed up. We returned to our rooms to consider our near-term future. (It didn't look good.)

While we were busy in the SAR with "training," someone had visited our rooms and carefully unmade the foot of our beds enough to slide out the mattress pad. Then they tidied up the foot of the bed good as new and placed the mattress pad on top of what looked like a perfect, inspection-ready bed. This heinous act required us to unmake, and then remake our beds to return the mattress pad to its rightful place. The shenanigans began bright and early the next morning. Powerful speakers were placed throughout the squadron. Why didn't we do this for calling minutes? Why didn't folks just look at their watches?

Beginning at about 00530 the speakers broadcast a heartbeat. It was barely audible at first but with time it gradually grew louder so that by 0600 you felt it more than you heard it. Right at 0600 the heartbeat stopped and a deafening alarm bell sounded. Simultaneously, our pals, the class of '79 exploded into our rooms shouting orders - Something about getting out of bed, what uniform to wear, and how we were going to die that day. Apparently, we were already late. (Well then, why didn't you wake us up earlier?)

After that warm and fuzzy start to the day, we formed up on the terrazzo and went for a little jog in the cool, thin Colorado morning air. Our run led us to a distinctive rock formation a mile or two north of the cadet area. Once there, we selected an appropriately shaped and sized rock (small boulder) and ran back to the squadron carrying the rock suspended in a blanket. At the squadron, we broke out the paint and brushes to decorate the rock in squadron and class colors. Someone in our class happened to have quite a bit of talent and did a striking job re-creating the CS-01 patch on the blue (our class color) rock. Tuesday morning was pretty much a repeat of Monday except for the rock painting.

Wednesday morning's run was fun because the end was only hours away. After the noon meal; AKA lunch, the cadet wing formed up on the terrazzo for our acceptance parade. We marched down to and took up position on the parade field. The cadet squadron commander faced the squadron and said, "Class of '79; fallout and make corrections!" For a second, my heart stopped. They marched us out here so they could kill and bury us on the spot, creating a new USAFA cemetery! But instead of jumping down our throats again, they shook our hook our hands and said, "Good job, Jonesy." Then they gave us our prop and wings which we immediately fixed to our flight caps.

My 38 year-old prop and wings are now proudly displayed in my retirement shadow box. There. Done. Thank God that's over. There were high-fives all around as we casually walked back up to Vandenberg Hall, purposefully avoiding the marble strips and using the elevator. Back in the squadron, I bought myself a Coke to soothe my sore throat and then I called my brother. (My parents were still overseas having left Naples for Sigonella, Sicily.) I told Rick, "It's over!" in a very raspy voice. What? It's over! You're drunk! You know better than that.

I was then and have always have been a nondrinker and I have never been drunk.

OCF

Heembo, Streif, and I stayed close throughout our USAFA years. We became involved with Officer Christian Fellowship (OCF), an organization promoting Christian values in the officer corps of all services world-wide. OCF had chapters at all the service academies but the one at USAFA was no doubt the premier chapter. We met every Friday evening at the home of either Major Bob and Diane Siegers or Lieutenant Commander Lee and Penny Wright. "Dad" Siegers was a peculiar guy (in a good way.)He was also a Christian Fighter pilot. He flew F-4s during Vietnam receiving the Silver Star. (A medal not easily earned in a jet.) He also had a goofy sense of humor. Here is his best known joke:

There once was a king potato and a queen potato

who had a beautiful little princess potato. The princess fell in love with and wanted to marry Walter Cronkite. But the king and queen potatoes wouldn't allow it because Walter was just a commentator. (common potato). We were also joined by Major Jim Woody and his wife Pat. Major Woody later became Brigadier General Woody, Deputy Commandant of Cadets, but I knew him when… Dick Brooks, an OCF executive also saw a lot of us. We studied the Bible, sang to guitars, (I learned to play after our regular guy graduated.) and enjoyed being away from the cadet area in a real home if even for only an hour or two on Friday evenings.

OCF had a fantastic retreat facility, named Spring Canyon tucked away in the Collegiate Range near Buena Vista Colorado. Spring Canyon was surrounded 14,000-foot peaks (each named after an Ivy-League school) near the continental divide. The main facility was a spacious log building, complete with stone fireplaces, a large meeting area, and the retreat's dining facilities. Visitors stayed in rustic log chalets scattered throughout the pine and aspen forest native to the region. In the winter months you expected snow measured in feet, not inches. Up the road an alpine lake reminiscent of Obernberg, seemed eternally frozen solid.

OCF was a welcome relief from the stresses of cadet life. Besides the nonsense described earlier, our academic load was enormous – (over twenty hours per semester was common). Another welcome relief for me came in the form of an absolutely too cute FSHS cheerleader, turned University of Northern Colorado student named Maureen Duff.

Dooly me, 1977

Neither of us remembers how we reconnected, but once we did, we saw a lot of each other. UNC was only an hour and a half north on I-25. Mo was popular in high school but we ran in different circles so we were really just acquaintances. That changed quickly in Colorado.

Today, "Mo" is a bold Christian and new grandmother.

The summer following my sophomore year, I participated in SERE (pronounced like the smart-phone app with all the answers) training.

SERE

SERE stands for Survival, Evasion, Resistance, and Escape. The premise of the training was:

We had been shot down in enemy territory and had only the contents of our aircrew survival kit on which to live while evading capture and navigating to friendly partisans who aided our evasion.

After several days of academics in the cadet Area, we were bussed out to the training area deep in the Colorado wilderness. At first we were divided into groups of about eight cadet trainees with one cadet instructor. We set up a common camp site, using a parachute to provide cover. Then the trainees built personal shelters out of materials nature provided and the parachute material and nylon cord that would have set us down. We built a new personal shelter each evening for the week we occupied the common camp site. Practice makes perfect, I suppose. It was like Boy Scouts; except we ate much better in scouts.

Our training included food aversion training which meant we ate things which humans don't normally eat. This is because the dry corn flake bars packed in our survival kits would last for decades packed away in our survival kits, but wouldn't last long, once opened.

We ate insects and whatever edible plants we could find. We also snared and ate a raven that made the mistake of visiting our little camp once too often. One evening our group was given a rabbit to eat. We knew a rabbit was coming but we didn't expect a big white fluffy bunny. We decided to name it, "Dinner." Someone was volunteered to kill the rabbit by clubbing it with a tree branch. We then we skinned and cooked Dinner on a spit over a wood fire. Dinner was quite tasty like most critters cooked over a wood charcoal fire, even hamsters, or was it guinea pigs?

To continue with the food aversion training, two of us had to swallow a pink eyeball. Four of us could have had a recently used rabbit's foot for good luck. I declined because, as you might recall, I don't believe in luck. Besides, Dinner had four and he wasn't very lucky, was he? (Tasty –yes, lucky –urp, you be the judge)

A day or two later the entire SERE class came together for a real treat – a small cow. The cow was dispatched humanely and then turned over to the trainees to take meat for making jerky. There was more food aversion training. You guessed it; a cow eyeball. The instructor cadre selected a volunteer whom they thought would be the most squeamish; in my class a female was presented an eyeball. Do you realize how big a cow eyeball is? It's too big to swallow whole like a rabbit's. You have to chew it first. Our poor volunteer nearly lost it when the eyeball exploded in her mouth, as did many of the spectators. Note to the curious: The lens of a cow's eye cannot be used as a magnifying glass to start fires, (I thought I'd give it a shot.), but it can be swallowed without chewing it up first. The cadre thought I should give *that* a shot. Back at our base camp, we used more parachute material and cord to make smokers for our strips of fresh beef. The result was some of the best beef jerky I've tasted. I loved it, and gladly traded away my corn flake bars for more. This would be my primary protein source for the upcoming trek.

The trek was three days and nights of travel from checkpoint to checkpoint using only a map and compass while aggressors (simulated enemy soldiers) searched for us. If caught, we were assessed points based on how grievous our errors were. Accumulate too many points and you had to repeat the training.

After this phase of SERE; we were loaded back on the busses with a surprise waiting for us. In each seat was a box lunch with a ham and cheese sandwich, a fried chicken breast, a Payday candy bar, and a can of Coke. No food aversion here! We were advised to go slow. Our stomachs had shrunk over the last two weeks and needed time to stretch back out. We were stuffed after a few bites.

Shortly after arriving back at the cadet area we were herded onto trucks and taken to another training area near Jack's Valley. This training area was a simulated POW camp. It was now time to train on resistance and escape. We were placed in narrow stalls with removable side slats to make them so narrow the sides pressed up against us. This was how we waited for our turn for interrogation. We had been given scenarios which included our aircraft type, unit, base, and our targets when we were shot down and captured. Our job was to resist giving up any of this information while being "tortured." They couldn't physically harm us so they simulated torture by putting us in "stress positions." For example, they had us go down on our knees on an incline with our knees pointed uphill. We then put our hands behind our heads and leaned backwards downhill, close to, but short of having our heads touch the back of our legs. After a minute or two our abs and thighs screamed for relief and cramped.

It was nothing compared to what our Vietnam POWs went through, but it was an effective simulation.

Later, we were placed in 4' x 4' cells with a coffee can for a toilet. We also had two pieces of 2" x 4s" nailed together to form a "T." This was our chair. We sat on the cross bar and balanced on the vertical piece. This was called the People's position and we were to remain in the People's position at all times which was difficult when all I wanted to do was lay down and sleep. If a guard found me off my little stool, I was dragged out and tortured. One technique the guards (many of whom were football players) used was to grab the lapels of our fatigue shirts and roll their fists into our chests. Then they shook us back and forth, pounding our chests with their fists. I witnessed one classmate of mine being lifted over the guard's head as he was shaken (not stirred) in this manner. This didn't hurt much but it left bruises on me. During this phase, fatigue due to sleep deprivation caught up with me. The camp's PA system constantly played Asian music. (Apparently we were still fighting in Viet Nam) The playlist included some songs with children singing. Once, I could have sworn the children singing were the Von Trapp kids singing *The Sound of Music* tunes. The following summer I volunteered to be a SERE survival instructor and enjoyed more time camping in Colorado.

My senior year suddenly appeared on the horizon and I had important decisions to make; like what kind of stone to select and what to inscribe in my class ring. I decided to go with "Philippians 4:13" for the inscription and a star sapphire as the stone.(Mom had one and it was cool.) It looks great.

William M. "Spike" Jones

R-L, Vandy, Koop, & I celebrate receiving
our USAFA class rings

Cadet first class me, fall 1978

The big decision concerned what I was going to do about a car. Several banks offered us great deals on car loans. I went with USAA Federal Savings Bank who offered six thousand dollars at three percent interest and we didn't have to start making payments until after graduation. We also had numerous dealerships that offered good deals. I called my father and said, "It's not Annapolis but it's free, so does your car offer still stand? He and Mom had recently returned to the states, bought a house, and were preparing for his pending retirement; so he back pedaled a bit and said," I didn't expect cars to cost as much as they do now, but how about this?" "You pick out the car you want, put your cadet loan down on it and I'll pay the difference." Any car?" I asked. "Any car." Okay, I'll give you six thousand dollars for the Mercedes. "Deal." He had trouble passing the Florida state inspection since the car wasn't built to US specs. I knew he was trying to sell it and I seized the opportunity. So my first car was a 1964 Mercedes-Benz 230 SL!

But wait, that's not extraordinary enough, there's more! When the car was shipped from Sicily to the States, It wound up in Norway rather than Norfolk over the winter months cracking the engine block. Since Uncle Sam shipped it; Uncle Sam put a new engine in it! Now that's extraordinary! My first car was a classic Mercedes-Bens sports car with a bland-new engine. More Grace? Of course, what else?

At USAFA the summer is divided into two three-week periods one period for training; the other for leave. During the summer after my dooly year (summer of '77) I attended the Army's Airborne training at Fort Benning, Georgia earning my jump wings. After Fort Benning, Heembo and I met at Charleston AFB, South Carolina to fly to Europe on a space-available basis. After a week of waiting; we gave up and went home – Tom to Michigan, me to Jacksonville. After using all my leave, I returned to Colorado to begin life as an upperclassman. In Michigan, Heembo got serious with Deb Behrens who would eventually married Tom a week before Shirley and I married.

Back at USAFA; I learned I had been assigned to CS-20, my home for the rest of my cadet days. CS-20 was on the fifth floor of Vandenberg Hall on the west end closest to Arnold Hall. We called ourselves the trolls which morphed into the tough, twenty trolls. Then in a moment of silliness, we became the terribly tenacious, tough, twenty trolls. Our mascot was Stan Lee's green Incredible Hulk which adorned our patch and a prominent wall at one end of the squadron. Our AOC was Captain William Begert, a former C-5 pilot. I later ran into Lieutenant General (three-stars) William Begert at Headquarters, US Air Forces Europe (USAFE). He was the vice commander. He didn't remember me.

Heembo was assigned to CS-33 in Sijan Hall. Sijan had carpeting (= no buffing floors) and sat next to Mitchell Hall or "Mitch's" the dining hall. Streif stayed in Vandenberg in CS-13.The three of us stayed close throughout our time at USAFA, due primarily to our participation in OCF.

Because we were together for three years, my friends and roommates in CS-20 were a big part of my success at USAFA. (I define success as graduating.) My closest friends were Chris Kupko (Koop); a local from Manitou Springs, and Tim Vandagriff (Vandy); a hilarious guy from Oklahoma.

On the terrazzo behind the flagpole, a black stone monument lists USAFA Graduates who have been killed in action over the years (The first class graduated in 1959.). Every time Vandy walked passed that monument; he saluted the names of the men engraved on it. This impressed me.

Vandy, Koop and I were shorter than the average cadet. The squadron called us the three munchkiteers (a blend of munchkins and musketeers). That let up some when Koop was appointed our squadron commander. We had another member of our vertically challenged team named Jeff Eggers from South Dakota. Jeff lost the end of his right index finger in a wheat harvesting accident; so, he came up a little short (pun intended) when we assumed the "All for One and One for All" pose.

Once, the Foosball table was discovered missing from the Foosball room. This was serious! We immediately suspected the rabble next door in CS-16, but after a thorough and lengthy investigation, we determined that Jeff and I moved it to our room for convenience. This saved us a dozen steps since our room was next to the foosball room. At 7258 feet plus five stories, every step counts.

Jeff left us early due to grades. Though he came up short (there it is again!) academically; he mastered the foosball table. Could there be a connection? Nope. Vandy, Koop and I were also masters on the Foosball table; Vandy and Koop were on the Superintendent's List (Dean's List plus Commandant's List). Me? No. I never threatened making Dean's List but I managed to stayed off academic probation. I made Commandant's List as a dooly in CS-01 and stayed on it until I graduated. As far as I know, I'm still on it! I still have the wreath I wore on my cadet uniform.

The heavily regimented lifestyle and enormous academic load caused us to make our own fun occasionally. For example, we invented a game called Frisbottle. Our Coke machine dispensed glass bottles. CS-20 had a long narrow hall.

To play Frisbottle; We stood two Coke bottles between twenty-five and thirty yards apart and attempted to knock them down with a Frisbee without touching a wall. Hitting the bottle on the fly earned three points. Landing and sliding the Frisbee into the bottle earned one point. Breaking the bottle ended the game until we swept up the glass and procured another bottle. A more extreme example was the time we Trolls flooded the men's shower room to play water polo. Someone removed and donated their closet door which we placed on its side across the entrance to the shower room. Wet toilet paper and paper towels created a seal around the door and plugged the drains in the floor. Next, we turned on the showers and in no time; CS-20 had an indoor, heated pool on the fifth floor of Vandenberg Hall. All was well until the seal around the door gave way and the water rushed into the restroom area outside the shower room. We quickly unplugged the drains but it didn't help much. Water raced under the mens room door and out into the hall giving it free access to the stairwell where gravity took over (Is this gravity thing a theme in my life?). We weren't worried about Captain Begert as much as we were about Jack, our janitor. If we messed up his clean hallway floors; we'd never hear the end of it. We enlisted the Doolies, (voluntarily, of course) who grabbed brooms and towels to guide the water into the stairwell and out of the squadron. After a long while the water dried up and we went to bed knowing both Jack and our AOC would know nothing about it.

We had organized official fun in the form of intramural sports; each squadron fielded teams for a plethora of sports.

Skiing USAFA, 1978

Academy intramural sports were extremely competitive considering the athletes involved were some of the best in their high schools. For example, I wrestled in the 131lbs. weight class for CS-01 as a dooly. At one match; I briefly wrestled the California state champion. I'd have spent more time with him if I'd have asked him for his autograph. Shortly after the referee started our contest, he tied me in a knot with my shoulders on the mat and my feet up in the air. We probably set some kind of record. I frequently had my bell rung when I played Lacrosse; a game I had never seen played. I held my own on the soccer team. I also played Team handball; a game of which I had never heard. I was pretty good at it until I broke my hand.

I had other roommates in CS-20 besides Vandy, Koop, and Jeff. Chuck Phillips was a very intelligent neat-freak who was later in my pilot training class as was Vandy. Ron Neilson was color blind, depending on his roommates to make sure he had the correct socks on.(Our uniform socks were black, not dark blue) I ran into Ron about 14 years after USAFA graduation at a kids' soccer game in Niceville, FL. I haven't seen Chuck or his wife, Mim since Pilot Training. Vandy and Koop attended our thirtieth re-union last fall. Vandy and his wife Cindy have twin sons who also attended USAFA.

After Pilot training, Vandy flew the C-130 Hercules and then flew for FedEx while flying C-130s for the Air National Guard on the side. Koop flew fighters after pilot training and later became an Operations Support Squadron commander (a tough job reserved for the best candidates available) at Davis-Monthom AFB, Arizona. He has since retired and moved his family back to Colorado. While in CS-20, the semesters came and went as did the Christmas, spring, and summer breaks that separated them. It was a long time coming but finally, I headed home for spring break 1979 to participate in Dad's retirement ceremony.

He called it quits after only thirty years. The ceremony was conducted in accordance with naval regulation and tradition. Rick and I were side boys and saluted crisply as Mom and Dad were piped overboard. Before Rick and I took our positions, I noticed an attractive young woman sitting in the audience. The white dress she wore accentuated her recently tanned and slightly burnt limbs. She sat with the Jacobs family. Chief Jacobs had recently retired after thirty years as well. After Dad's ceremony, many came back to the house in nearby Orange Park for the obligatory retirement party. After the fourth time hearing Jonny Paycheck's rendition of *Take this Job and shove it*, I asked Shirley and Teresa if they wanted to leave to go do something. They were agreeable so we hopped into the 230SL and went to the Putt-putt Golf Course on Blanding Boulevard. On the way back to the Jacobs house in Normandy Village, we stopped by a McDonalds. Shirley hopped in the booth and sat down beside me. She sat close enough for our knees to touch, an unmistakable sign of interest! At the Jacobs' house; Teresa bolted from the car as soon as I switched off the *new* engine. (Good thing the top was down) She ran inside leaving Shirley and me alone. We agreed to go to the beach together the next day. I picked her up early and we spent most of the day at Jax Beach. That evening, Shirley and I shared our first kiss when I took her home on Fouraker Road.

Shirley was sitting on the fender of the Mercedes as Teresa watched through the window by the front door. She was happy to share with the family how I was "kissing on Shirley" in the drive way. Spring break ended and I returned to Colorado. But I didn't stay gone long. I was home on summer leave soon. Shirley and I picked up where we left off, spending every possible moment together. I attended her Ed White high school graduation along with the rest of the Jacobs clan. I was still on Fouraker Road late that night, after the graduation party when Shirley and I decided to go to the beach to spend the remaining few hours of the night and watch the sun rise on her first day after high school. After telling Miss Jean our plan; rather than nix it like I expected, she went to the kitchen and packed some food for us to take. Was she pushing her daughter off on me? If so, it worked. A week later, on June 12th, I asked Shirley to be my wife. She agreed.

Shirley & me in St. Augustine, Dec 1979

The next morning the headlines reported John Wayne's death. We (Shirley) set the date for June 14th (Flag Day) 1980; about two weeks after my USAFA graduation. While driving my car from Florida to Colorado, it dropped its transmission in Fort Worth, Texas. That cost me a bundle because it forced me to fly on up to C Springs and back to pick up the car after it was fixed. Then, when I stopped at a car wash in C Springs before going up to the Cadet Area, it wouldn't start. What kind of lemon did my Dad stick me with?! I called a repair service and the guy asked if it had been tuned for altitude yet. That answer cost me $200. Then the alternator needed to be replaced a month or two later - another $300, please. It occurred to me that I might not be able to afford to maintain this old car.

My First Car, 1979

I sold it for $10,000. Then I went to a Mazda dealer. They were out of RX-7s so I paid cash for a new little hatchback; the GLC (great little car) and put the rest of the money I made on the Mercedes in a CD.

The typical cadet car included Corvettes, Camaro Z-28s, Trans-Ams, and the like. I fit right in with my little econobox. I got even one wintry evening, though.

The road leading up to Vandenberg Hall is fairly steep. The typical cadet car with their wide tires found no traction on the slushy climb to the best parking slots under the dorm. The hill was littered with American muscle. But my Japanese GLC with its skinny little tires and great gas mileage motored right up that hill. It *was* a great little car! (More Grace!)

May 28th 1980 dawned clear and bright – just like my future. After Dad swore me in as a second Lieutenant; I threw my hat in the air at Falcon Stadium as the USAF Aerial demonstration Team, better known as the Thunderbirds flew overhead. Gold bars – check; diploma – check. Stick a fork in me, I'm done! It's time to hit the road.

I had to drive back to Jacksonville.

USAFA graduation, 28 May 1980

Then Shirley and I had to drive to Michigan with overnight stops in Atlanta and the Freese home in Ohio. Then after Tom and Deb's June 7th wedding, we drove back down to Jacksonville to tie our own knot one week later. Shirley planned a medium-sized wedding in Normandy Park Baptist Church. Neither of us had ever attended this church before our wedding, but it had a center aisle – a must for Shirley. Her Youth Pastor, at Westside Baptist Church, Bucky Burney, performed the ceremony.

Bucky was quite the character. I suppose all youth pastors have to be a little quirky to keep the kids interested, but Bucky was exceptionally quirky. As a second job, he flew F-106s for the Florida Air National Guard. Like Maverick, he had a history of unauthorized flyovers at birthday parties, high school football games, and USAFA. He was also the best water-skier I ever saw outside of the professionals at Cypress Gardens.

The Navy couldn't decide if Rick was going to be deployed or not; so I had two best men - Rick and Tom. Groomsmen; Larry, Vandy, and Koop rounded out my side of the wedding party.

L to R; Larry, Koop, me, Heembo, Rick, Vandy

Andy, son of LCDR Lee & Penny Wright from OCF was our ring barer. With this crowd, the rehearsal was a hoot and the ceremony *almost* came off without a hitch.

Shirley was shaking nervously when Jake brought her down the aisle to me. "Relax, we can do this," I told her quietly.

Then the trinity candle part of the ceremony ambushed us. The script called for Shirley and I to remove the burning candles on our respective sides of the candle holder and simultaneously light the center candle. But, these were not the wax candles with which we rehearsed. They were hollow, metal tubes shaped like candles with internal springs to continuously expose fresh wick for extended burning time. Shirley had her candle out of its holder and ready to go immediately. This girl was anxious!

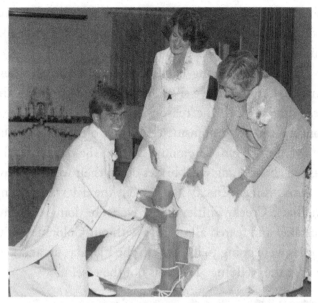

Jean, Shirley& me, Jun 1980

My candle, however, didn't cooperate. Its base was stuck in the holder. This was not a show-stopper. I would just use both hands to wrestle it free. I grabbed the base of the candle and tried to twist it out. This was the exact wrong technique. What I accomplished was to disconnect the metal shaft of the candle from its base which remained stuck to the holder as if welded (or super-glued, Vandy!). At this point the spring took over the ceremony and launched the candle stick off the holder. The spring kept it from being catapulted into the audience like a fiery medieval siege weapon but it remained attached to the candle shaft which was bouncing up and down with the appropriate springy sound effect. Great – a little levity to break the tension can be a good thing. Shirley, my beautiful teenage bride, stood there holding her candle stoically, a *with what the heck is your* problem? look on her face. I responded with my best; *I meant to do that* face, and took Shirley's hand in mine as we lit the middle candle like this was how it's supposed to be done.

Then, after racing back up the aisle, people threw bird seed at us and we sped away in our decorated, can-dragging GLC. One reason Shirley was nervous was concern for my groomsmen and me. Shirley scheduled an evening (7 pm) ceremony. During the day while she rushed about doing what brides do on their wedding day; my groomsmen, Bucky and I spent the day water skiing on Black Creek. Shirley knew we were doing this (my mistake) and feared all us guys with our Colorado white bodies were going to burn up in the Florida sun and keel over at the wedding. This was not the case.

Dealing with wedding day jitters, Jun 1980

CHAPTER VI
PILOT TRAINING

Our honeymoon was quick and inexpensive. The money I made on the Mercedes sale purchased furniture for our apartment, which, we stored in my parent's garage until the movers loaded it for the long haul to Oklahoma. The driver made great time and we soon learned we could accept delivery as soon as we could get there. So off we sped yet again in our GLC bound for Vance AFB in Enid, Oklahoma. On a previous trip from Colorado, Shirley and I found a new two-bedroom apartment in tiny Waukomis, OK about five miles south of the base We settled in and Shirley found a job immediately at Waukomis State Bank across the street. Tom and Deb Heemstra moved into the apartment next door while Chuck and Mim Phillips had an apartment on the first floor beneath the Heemstras. Another member of class 8108 lived in the apartment under ours. She was a 1st Lieutenant with a huge chip on her shoulder named, Dee Gillis. After some ground training and academics our class was divided into two sections of about thirty students each to make our schedule more manageable. Everyone at the Chisholm Trail Apartments wound up in the same section making carpooling easier.

Oklahoma was seriously hot. For fun, we often sat outside the apartment building in lawn chairs waiting for the temperature on the bank's sign to go below 100° F. During our time in Waukomis, Enid set a record for the number of consecutive days over 100° F. Oklahoma was also very windy – so windy, all the trees leaned north because of the strong hot wind coming up from Texas. Outside felt like a blow dryer.

Undergraduate Pilot Training (UPT) lasted fifty-two weeks; the first six months were spent flying the exceedingly loud, slow, uncomfortable, slow, and quite loud T-37.What the Tweet lacked in airspeed, it more than made up for in volume.

2x T-37s from Sheppard AFB, Air Force
photo courtesy, Harry Toneman

The last six months, were flown in the sleek, supersonic, sexy T-38.

A 560 FTS T-38, Air Force photo courtesy, Jo Hunter

Follow-on aircraft were assigned a few weeks before graduation based on our performance.

A computer-derived timeline drove our lives. To have the number of students in our class graduate on time required twelve-hour days. They began early enough to conduct an hour-long mass briefing, which ended at least an hour before the first scheduled event. We alternated between early-week and late-week. On early –week, simulator sorties preceded flying sorties which launched beginning at sunrise so mass briefing show times could be as early as 0330.

On Late weeks days started so that the mass brief ended an hour before the first aircraft sortie launch at sunrise. Then following a full day of flying; simulator sorties wrapped up the day before we were released, twelve hours after our show time. We typically walked back to the squadron from the simulator building in the dark.

The most stressful time of UPT occurred during the

mass briefing. One IP in the flight was designated the unit standardization and Evaluation member (USEM). His job was to make sure we students could handle any aircraft malfunction in the event it happened when we were solo. During the mass brief he took the podium and described a situation. for example, "You're in area 5 low over the town of Lahoma at 12,000 feet and 200 knots with your nose 20 degrees down accelerating at 100% power, setting up for a Cloverleaf when you see a flashing red light in the right fuel shut-off T-handle." The class held its breath because the USEM next selected a victim by saying, "Lt Vandagriff, You have the aircraft." Then poor Vandy stood up with his checklist and in-flight guide in hand to described in detail how he would accomplish the basics of: 1) Maintain aircraft control. 2) Analyze the situation and take the appropriate action. And 3) Land as soon as conditions permit. Vandy could use anything available to him in the aircraft like his local area map and afore mentioned checklist and in-flight guide to resolve the given situation – with one exception.

Some emergency situations require action so promptly that referring to a checklist is not practical. These procedures are written in boldface type in the book. They were memorized verbatim. On written boldface tests, a missing comma fails. During the mass brief or debriefing after a flight, a stutter fails. Failing boldface was a grounding offense. If the selected student fails to handle his emergency properly, he was sat down grounded for the day. The situation could be handed -off at any time so everyone paid close attention. If a follow-on student messed up and was sat down, he too was grounded and another victim was selected. It was possible for a half a dozen or more students to be grounded in one mass briefing. If we performed poorly like this as a class we might be put back on formal release; ensuring we'd have more time to study and quiz each other on emergency procedures. Heembo, Vandy, Chuck, Dee, and I were assigned to C Flight in the 8th Flying Training Squadron (FTS). (Remember this.) The flight room walls were lined with tables extending from the wall into the room. (One for each IP) There were also several tables pushed together in the center of the room. Three students were typically assigned to each IP. At one end of the room was a large counter behind which was a wall containing the day's schedule. On each side of the schedule hung computer print outs indicating anything the scheduler needed to know about a student's syllabus activities.

UPT is conducted by categories; first in sequence is contact flying where the weather allows the student to see the horizon to maintain proper aircraft attitude and ground references for navigation. This category emphasized patterns and landings (normal and emergency) and in the working areas; stalls and spin recoveries. Yes, IPs actually put the aircraft into a full stall or spin and had us recover. The idea was to teach us how to get out of any trouble in which we might find ourselves when solo.

The next category was Formation. One aircraft leads while the other maintains position from close formation (three- feet wingtip spacing) to extended trail formation where the wingman flies several hundred feet away while the lead aircraft flies aerobatics. Formation flying is fundamental to fighter aircraft so the student who performed well in this category highlights himself as one to watch for the remainder of the course.

The Navigation category included navigation via navigational aids and instruments as well as map reading. This phase included out and back sorties to other air fields and a weekend-long cross country series of flights. It also included a low-level sortie were we flew at one thousand feet using only a map and a clock to fly over a "target" at our assigned time plus or minus thirty seconds. Staying on course in the blustery Oklahoma winds was a challenge.

The last category was Instruments where we flew published approaches without any outside visual references to within a few hundred feet of the runway and then transitioned to a landing. The simulator was a perfect training aid for this, but there is no substitute for the real thing. By positioning our visor covers just so, our vision was restricted to the instrument panel. To simulate breaking out of the clouds, the IP reached over and tore away the Velcro-attached visor cover. Overhead patterns and landings were revisited in the Instrument/ Navigation categories to the peril of students with retention difficulties.

C Flight in the 8th had a tradition of recognizing buffoonery. If a student committed a bufoonerous act, he was nominated for the "block" award at the end of the day. The nominator wrote and read a poem describing the egregious behavior and the IPs voted whether the act and the poem were worthy of the block o' shame which sat on the offender's IP's desk until the recipient learned of some other offense and passed the award along.

On one sortie, my stomach disagreed with me enough

that I needed to empty it. No problem; I'll just pull my trusty airsick bag out of my flight suit's leg pocket where I always kept it and…oops my pocket was empty! So with no bag available; I improvised and threw up in my oxygen mask which was secured to my face as it should have been.

Ever try to fit three quarts of soup into a one quart container? The oxygen mask was designed to seal around the face to keep air from escaping; not soup at high pressure, so out it came with surprising velocity. I helped the crew chief clean the cockpit before the next aircrew arrived. Someone must have seen me and tattled.

After cleaning myself up in the mens room, I noticed Al Matter (another 8108/I member) and my pal, Dee Gillis, huddled together at a table in the snack bar. Dee was writing furiously while they both snickered. Something's up. After debriefing the sortie, I worked on my own poem, just in case.

Sure enough; When C Flight assembled for formal release, Dee nominated me for the block award. The poem and my buffoonery where pretty funny so after the IPs voted, I stepped up on the platform to receive the block. "Is it too soon to give it away?" Yeah, right many scoffed thinking it impossible for me to have rooted out buffoonery so quickly. "No, really," I said as I whipped a piece of paper out of my pocket:

Instead of a bag, to use my mask;
I admit was a particularly disgusting task
But something even more disgusting to do;
Is to have someone else write your poem for you;
Come on, Dee we know you're not dumb;

We've all seen you walk and chew gum
When you're out in the jet doing spins, loops, and stalls
Will Al Matter be making your radio calls?

I can't remember any more but it was a big hit with the IPs and my fellow students. Dee became the new owner of the block but she didn't allow me to hand it over. When the room cheered their approval; her eyes filled with tears and she left, slamming the flight room door, stranding her carpoolers. That evening at home, Dee's stereo was cranked so loud our floor shook.

Besides Dee making a spectacle of herself, I witnessed some additional excitement while flying solo in the T-37 pattern at Vance. A T-38 landed short of the runway. The wheels dug into the dirt enough that when the plane came to the runway's edge, the right landing gear sheared off causing the plane to roll over on its back and slide down the runway inverted. In the T-38, the IP in the back seat sits higher than the student up front. The IP in this accident was killed instantly while the student was severely injured.

With the last T-37 sortie flown; class 8108 moved next door to M Flight of the 25th FTS to fly the much faster T-38.

I considered myself a late-bloomer. I was average in the T-37 but for some reason, I excelled in the T-38. I remember laughing out loud the first time I felt the afterburners kick in. My IP, Captain Doug Spears, was very laid-back and I performed well for him. The T-38 phase was of training was nearly identical to the T-37 phase with the same categories but more formation flying and faster low-levels. Our time in T-38s was not without excitement.

8108 classmate, Julie Thie became the first woman to eject from an aircraft when she and her IP punched out of their burning T-38 shortly after take-off. The plane came down on Enid's north side leaving scrape marks across Willow Road, before coming to rest and burning in someone's backyard. No one was hurt.

Near the end of the T-38 phase; we filled out "dream sheets" to let the Air Force Personnel Center (AFPC) know which aircraft we wanted to fly following UPT, listed in order of preference. How well you finished compared to your classmates determined how far down the list they went to give you an assignment. It was nice of them to create the illusion that we had some say in the matter but the truth was that the needs of the Air Force took priority over the wishes of naïve young lieutenants. That's why they're called *dream sheets*, duh! We were told all the first assignment IP (FAIP) positions were filled by volunteers, so none of us needed to worry about sticking around to teach after graduation. Why wouldn't that be true, if that's what they told us? Without bothering to talk to any fighter pilots in the wing; or anyone with a clue, I elected to list the RF-4 as my first choice and the FB-111 as my second choice. I chose these because they were high performance aircraft located at only a few bases world-wide. I figured this would mean less moving around for the family. I knew I wanted to fly high performance jets but didn't list our front-line fighters like everyone else because I didn't think I was competitive for one. But God had a better plan. *He always does.*

I chuckled in amazement, today at a small gift God gave me earlier. The Chamberlin Hotel sits on Fort Monroe in the city of Hampton on the southern tip of the Virginia peninsula. The body of water it fronts is known as Hampton Roads, at the south end of the Chesapeake Bay. Civil War history buffs should recognize the name. This is where the ironclads, Monitor and Merrimac duked it out. Today, Hampton Roads is one of the busiest ports in the world. Norfolk Naval Station is visible to the south. I can see aircraft carriers and other warships moored at Pier 12 from my back door. I see call manner of Naval vessel every day. As they leave, I say a prayer for the safety of the crew and the sad families still at the pier or driving home without Dad.

I've appointed myself the unofficial harbor monitor on Ft Monroe. Earler today I was making my required morning survey from the Ft Monroe seawall and witnessed a dazzling specticle only God could have arranged for me. I have always enjoyed the sight of the sun shimmering off a body of water. Today's display was particularly magnificent. As I sat mezmerized by the sight, I thought of what it took to create such a brilliant, beautiful display.

First, the water had to be relatively flat and calm with only a gentle breeze to create the required ripples. Then the sun had to be at just the right height above the horizon. Did not God, specifically, Jesus demonstrate his power to control the wind and the waves my merely saying, "Peace, be still?" (Matthew 8:24) And in the Old testament, didn't God demonstrate his power over all His creation by stopping the sun?(Joshua 10:12) and even backing it up as a sign to King Hezekiah that He would extend his life as promised? (2Kings 20:11)

So, who else could have given me such a treat today? Why? Because He knows I like it and it pleased Him to please me. Its another glimpse of grace. His grace is everywhere if you know Him and know where to look.

With graduation only weeks away and our dream sheets filled-out; UPT class 8108 excitedly waited for our Assignment Night at the Officer's Club. We were told that the eleven IP assignments coming down for our class were already filled with volunteers, so *no one should be surprized* to be returning to Vance to teach UPT after graduation. I repeat this because it's important. In all truth, to be selected as a FAIP(first assignment IP) should be considered a positive, because the squadron to which you were being assigned knew you and wanted you back.

Assignment Nights were a big deal – a huge, well attended party that usually had some kind of theme to make it more fun. We had a wheel of Fortune with all the aircraft in the AF inventory on it in their proper proportion. When a student's picture(usually an embarassing, childhood photo or a current, unflattering picture) was shown; the student put a five dollar bill in a large bowl, took the stage, and gave the wheel a spin. Then the student's assignment was projectected. If the assignment matched the wheel, the student won the money in the bowl at the end of the night. Remember, 8108 had 60 students so the bowl would have enough cash by the end of the night to make a couple happy.

Colonel Giles D. Harlow, Commander, 71st Flying Training Wing (who already knew the aircraft drop for our class), attempted to do the unnecessary- fire up the already well- lit crowd.

He said ours was the best aircraft drop he'd ever seen!

And he's been at Vance since the Wright brothers! The crowd went wild. Our drop had the least number of engines he'd ever seen!(Fewer engines meant more fighters and fewer bombers, tankers, and transport aircraft.)The crowd went wilder. *"ALL BUT TWO OF YOU got one of your top three choices"!* This was unheard of! Are you people getting this?! We were giddy with delight and couldn't wait to get this thing started. I told Shirley, "I should have asked for an Eagle." (the F-15)

Then they started handing out the assignments and it was like Christmas. Life-long dreams were being realized and the bowl was filling up. I kept telling Shirley, "I should have asked for an eagle!" Finally, my naked baby picture appeared. I dropped my money in the bowl, and took the stage to spin the wheel. I gave it a spin and it stopped on a Phantom.(the F-4) Yeehaw! I was getting my first choice *AND* the money! Just Kidding, Jonesy.

Then they projected my real assignment but it wasn't an F-4! *What is that?* I was standing too close to the screen. I couldn't focus on the jet. All I saw was a white blur(back then, all training command jets were white) and the audience joined me in a collective, "Augh" of disapointment followed by complete silence. We were all stunned! I was going to be a T-38 FAIP! I had no clue it was coming. *But you said all the FAIP assignments had volunteers!* I didn't volunteer! All my classmates were realizing dreams come true except Jery Siegel and me.(We were the "two who didn't get one of our top three choices." I was devistated. As was the custom; the 25th FTS commander joined me on stage, shook my hand, gave me a bottle of champagne, and placed a blue, star-spangled squadron scarf around my neck. I was so upset, Shirley had to drive us back to Waukomis. Could we survive another three years in this hot, hot, tornado-plagued place?

What about Dee? I'm glad you asked. Back then, women weren't allowed to fly fighters so Dee volunteered to be a T-38 IP. The 25th FTS determined she was not IP-qualified, which meant they didn't want her so she was assigned a C-141; a large cargo aircraft with a crew she'd have to figure out how to get along with. This left a T-38 IP slot open for me. Thanks, Dee!

I never saw nor heard of her again. During the few weeks remaining until graguation, I felt like I was stuck in Pilot Training while my friends and classmates were happily preparing to go fly in the real Air Force. August 26th 1981 eventually arrived and we received our silver wings. Dad pinned mine on. In keeping with tradition, Vandy and I broke a set of wings and exchanged halves. I was still struggling with the faip thing and had to remind myself that *God is in control* and regardless of what was happening to me, it was part of His plan for my life. (Read: Shut up and color, Lt. Jones.)

But first- more training. I flew commercial to Miami for the Air Force water survival course at Homestead AFB, FL. We parasailed off one of the few ships in the Air Force inventory; and sat in our little one-man life rafts in the middle of the turqoise waters of Biscayne Bay until a helicopter came to lift us out of the drink. After a few days to dry off at home, I departed for San Antonio, Texas and Pilot Instuctor Traning(PIT) at Randolph AFB.

It was November 4th 1981(I don't know why I rememberthat date). I was filling up my car at the base gas station up for the long drive south when I heard the tornado sirens. I looked west and beyond the rows of T-38s a tornado descended out of the clouds. I took a picture of it and left for San Antonio.

PIT was similar to pilot training except we received two grades for every maneuver. One for proficiency from the backseat(It's hard to see from back there.) and one for instruction. The days weren't near as long and we lived in the bachelor officer quarters instead of our homes. The food dining out was also better. San Antonio food is hard to beat especially if you know a ocal to show you where the good places are. I did. Lori Schmitt was a good friend fron Naples. She was a'76 classmate at FSHS and attended my church. She was active with the youth group so I also knew her from Tuesdays at the villa and the church camp. Lori and Nibor were close friends. Lori's Parents owned a real estate business just outside the main gate at Randolph AFB.

PIT progressed along without any hiccups and I earned my IP rating in about five months. Heembo volunteered to be a T-37 faip and was going through T-37 PIT at the same time. He and I met Shirley, and Deb in Dallas for an occasional weekend rendezvous. This helped greatly in getting through the five month - long separation. After completing another series of category check rides(I hate those things.); I was a qualified T-38 IP. I drove back up to Waukomis and hung my shingle up in G Flight of the 25th FTS. I worked for Captain Dave Jankowski, an experienced F-4 fighter pilot and T-38 IP. I liked his style.

CHAPTER VII

T-38 FAIP LIFE IN
THE BACK SEAT

Shortly after returning from PIT, Shirley and I were offered base housing; so we gathered some friends together (the ones with trucks and trailers) and moved ourselves into a duplex on Edwards Street. After installing a fence for the dog, we were good to go.

In the back seat of a 25 FTS T-38

Did I forget to mention the dog?

Like all *good* Americans, I am a dog person. Cats aren't worth the match it takes to set them on fire. Growing up, we always had a dog or two; never a cat, once a parakeet, and for a short time, a hamster. (Or was it a guinea pig?)

Back in Pilot Training, John and Linda Owens discovered their Irish setter, Lady, was pregnant. This was because another 8108 classmate, Dave Desboard, had a male Irish setter named Duke. Dave was a bachelor and pets were not allowed in the Bachelor Officer Quarters (BOQ). John and Linda helped Dave out and let Duke stay in their fenced-in yard on base with Lady, unchaperoned. In May of '81, John came into the flight room looking for anyone who wanted a puppy. "How much are you asking for them, John?" I asked. "Nothing, I just want to get rid of the things." I have always loved the look of Irish setters. "Let me talk to Shirley, but I'm pretty sure we'll take one." Shirley agreed so I told John we'd definitely take one. We'd figure a way around that pesky, no pets policy at the apartment, later.

Linda hosted an 8108 wives get together when Lady went into dog labor. (Whelping? I think.) Shirley called me and I rushed right over to witness the miracle of life. Lady had a litter of ten healthy red puppies that evening. One female had a little white on one of her front toes. John told me, since I was first to commit, I could have pick of the litter. They all looked alike so I chose the white-toed female thinking it would be easier to find her after the litter spent eight weeks with Lady. We named her Kelly and she was a blessing.

Shirley was anxious to start a family but it wasn't happening for us so in a very small way, Kelly filled that void. I had no idea what an intense desire childbearing can be for a woman and conversely, how agonizing infertility can be. Hopes were dashed every month. When word came from home that a friend or cousin was pregnant, it hurt Shirley. Walking through department stores with baby clothes, furniture, and accessories hurt so badly we avoided them. Shirley looked into adoption but the military's mobile lifestyle was a hindrance. The adoption process can be lengthy and it looked doubtful we'd ever be in one place long enough. The medical community offered no hope. We both had plumbing issues we tried correcting with surgery but it didn't help.

Hiding an eight week-old puppy wasn't hard. But we made the mistake of feeding her and she grew.

Shirley, Kelly & me 1981

She was adorable and wanted everyone to know it. She had long, difficult to control legs and boundless energy. While going downstairs to go outside she introduced herself to the apartment manager. Busted!

Soon she flew to Jacksonville to grow up a bit on Fouraker Road until we could pick her up to live with us on base at Vance. That time came the following Christmas. Shirley and I drove from Enid to Jacksonville to surprise my family and pick up Kelly.

We first stopped at the house on Fouraker road where Kelly met us at the door. She was fat! Evidently, she had been spoiled rotten as the first grand dog. After celebrating the holidays, we returned to Vance and put Kelly on a diet. She turned out to be an intelligent animal.

She was very easy to train and loved to play hide and seek with a knotted sock. We had her sit and stay in the living room while we disappeared to the back of the house to hide it. She sat patiently until we told her to go get her sock. Then she searched the house until she found it. Shirley taught her to retrieve the morning paper so she could stay inside on cold mornings. Northern Oklahoma could get very cold as well as very hot and the wind was a constant any time of year. Promotion to 1Lt is determined by the calendar so when my time as a 2Lt was up, I went to the exchange and purchased my silver bars. This small pay increase plus the housing allowance we'd receive if we moved off base should cover the mortgage on a small place and we'd have a home of our own. We found a nice little starter home on West Cherokee Street. It was surrounded by wheat fields (where Kelly loved to run.)The base was a short drive away. (Everything was a short drive away in

Enid!) To give use a little more breathing room financially, Shirley found a good job at a small oil company named, Sunburst Energy. Sunburst owned and operated the equipment to drill oil wells. If someone thought they might be sitting over an oil deposit, they'd pay Sunburst to drill the hole and find out. Striking oil or not (known as a dry hole) Sunburst got paid. Shirley has the gift of organization so she did very well as the president's personal secretary and the company payroll manager.

CHAPTER VIII

BACK TO THE FRONT SEAT

On paper, FAIPs look alike. Opportunities to stand out are few. After almost two years in the 25th, I was still a line IP. I was in the Runway Supervisory Unit (RSU) Program (the team of instructors who controlled the very busy overhead pattern). I also had a good additional duty (assistant USEM) in G Flight. But when less than exciting assignments came down for guys with more with which to compete than me, I decided to buy myself some more time and volunteered teach PIT at Randolph AFB in San Antonio, TX.

In January 1984, I hitched our sailboat, *Dixie* (an O'Day 22) to the car and Shirley, Buffy (a pretty but stupid Cocker Spaniel we picked up), Kelly, and I headed South, down I-35. I was able to quickly get a mooring on beautiful Canyon Lake in the Texas Hill Country; about forty minutes from the house Lori helped us find in Converse, close to the base.

Keeping the boat in the water meant having to pull her out to clean her hull every other weekend, but it was great to just take a taxi boat or swim out to her, raise the sails, and be on our way without having to raise the mast, rig, and launch her. We particularly enjoyed taking dinner out to the lake with us along with new crew "take it down" Darrell (he mistakenly raised the genoa upside-down once.) and Christie Brandon. We ate dinner (not the rabbit) on the water and sailed until after dark, and then felt our way back to the marina.

For no apparent reason, things happened for me as a PIT instructor in the 560th FTS. First, after some time on the line, I became a Check pilot. This meant I no longer worked out of D Flight with students assigned to me. Instead, I flew category check rides. Then; shortly after receiving my certificate for completing Squadron Officer School (SOS) by correspondence, I was selected to attend SOS in-residence, which was a very good thing.

Shortly after settling in Converse, Shirley saw a TV commercial about adoptions sponsored by Lutheran Social Services (LSS) of Texas. She called the number on the screen and learned LSS paired infertile couples with women in crisis pregnancies. We filled out an application and were accepted into their program which was big on education. We read books, talked with counselors, participated in round-table discussions about the adoption triangle: the adoptee, the *birth* mother, (not real mother or natural mother) and the adoptive parents.

In the past, due to the stigma that used to be attached to adoption, most adoption records were sealed to protect the privacy of the participants. LSS provided open adoptions where the triangle members meet each other and mutually agree to how much family information is to be shared and with how much contact everyone is comfortable.

In our case, Shirley and I filled out background forms and answered questions about our religious beliefs and how we intended to raise our baby. All the couples in our group did this. Then LSS screened the applications to match them up with what the birth mothers in the program indicated the kind of people they wanted to parent their babies. Then the birth mother chose the adoptive parents and on placement day, placed the baby in the adoptive parents' arms.

The hardest form to fill out was the form indicating what we would accept in a child; we were given about every possible racial or ethnic combination and had to check a box for yea or nay. We did the same for scores of possible birth defects. Then we continued with birthmother behavior/pregnancy circumstances such as prenatal smoking, alcohol abuse, light marijuana use, heavy marijuana use, heroin, cocaine, LSD, and prescription drug abuse. How about a pregnancy due to rape and/or incest? How about twins or triplets or more? These were gut wrenching questions to consider. We wanted to increase our chances for adoption while protecting ourselves from heartbreak. If we had indicated that we wanted a defect-free, blonde-haired, blue-eyed baby boy from a clean birthmother, we'd still be waiting.

At some point in the process, we learned we had been chosen by a birth mother but were not told her due date. Shirley did her decorating magic and turned our guestroom into a beautiful nursery appropriate for either gender. (We could have picked that, too.) All we needed was a baby. Any time the phone rang, it could be *the call*.

But the call didn't come right away and I had to leave for eight weeks of SOS at Maxwell AFB in Montgomery, Alabama. 560th buddy, Phil Finch, of Cabot, Arkansas, was in the same class so we drove out together. The class was divided into flights. Phil and I were also in the same flight.

On the first day (a Monday), our flight gathered in a classroom to get to know each other. We were instructed to write our names on a card on our desk to help everyone learn them. I complied immediately, writing Mike Jones on my name card. Phil picked it up and read it repeatedly aloud to himself, "Mike Jones," "Mike Jones," etc. as if contemplating its deeper meaning. "You know; that's real close to Spike Jones;" "Yes sir, *Spike Jones and his City Slickers*". Spike Jones was a comedic band leader in the late 40s and early 50s who performed parodies of popular songs of the day.

Phil wrote Spike Jones on my name card and it's been Spike Jones ever since. Many USAF friends don't know me by any other name. One squadron commander told me to put Spike on my flight suit nametag (technically a no-no) so he wouldn't be confused.

On Friday of that first week of SOS, the flight was socializing at our flight commander's home, when the phone rang. My flight commander answered it. "Spike, it's for you." Oh no, who died? We all thought. I also thought, how did anyone know I was here and how did they get the number? It must be something serious. Phones don't ring at times like this unless it's bad news. Shirley was on the line sounding very shook up. I'm still thinking someone's died. "Michael," she said, (this *was* serious. (She only calls me Michael when it's serious.) "They have a little girl for us, "She was born yesterday and we can pick her up Monday. "Do we want her?" "Of course we want her!" After I hanged up everyone looked at me to find out who died. I said," I'm a father!" "We didn't even know you were pregnant, Spike!" Then I turned to my flight commander. "I need to take some leave."

Early the next morning, I sped off to the south towards I-10 while an angry lady named Helena ambled north. Hurricane Helena was taking aim at Alabama's Gulf coast. It was a race to see who would get to I-10 first. I won. I took a right on I-10 West, toward Texas.

Shirley and I spent our last childless weekend together. We went to LSS in downtown San Antonio at the appointed time on Monday and Laura's birth mother, a sixteen year-old high school student placed a beautiful four day-old baby girl in our arms. It had been nine months since Shirley saw that commercial on TV and called LSS (Coincidence?).

After a brief chapel ceremony, we took our daughter home to meet her dogs. God was gracious again. Laura was perfect and beautiful. She'd say she still is. So would her husband. I agree.

We recently celebrated her 29th birthday. I officially feel old, now.

Back to 1985 - People stopped Shirley in stores to tell her what beautiful baby she had and comment on how quickly she had lost her pregnancy weight.

Shirley & Laura, 1985

They also said Laura must look like her father. Isn't it silly - the strange things people will say to perfect strangers because of babies? Laura's birth mother is Caucasian and colored much like Shirley and me. Her birth father is Mexican giving Laura hair and eyes so dark brown, they almost look black and a beautiful complexion.

Like Kelly, we fed her (not dog food) and she grew. She became a rough and tumble toddler who grew into quite the little athlete.

Laura taking charge

When I returned to the squadron after SOS, I found IP of the Month and IP of the Quarter plaques in my inbox. The secret to my success was apparently being absent. Despite my presence, I also won 12 FTW IP of the Year, 1985.

Laura was beyond bright. Later, she was placed in the talented and gifted program in elementary school. On the school's recommendation we had her tested and she came up two points shy of genius. Two points! - What a little slacker! We weren't surprised; we knew she was very bright when she memorized C. Clement Moore's *A Visit From St. Nick*. ('Twas the night before Christmas...) in its entirety at 3 ½ years-old.

In early 1986, I was preparing to watch *TOPGUN* at a theater in Universal City; when 560th friend, Jay

Escude (snail) asked me if I had talked to our squadron commander that afternoon before I went home. I said no, I hadn't. Jay said, you need to call the boss right now. "Now?" I asked. "Right now", he insisted. So I went to the lobby and found a pay phone to call Lt Col Scott McCabe, my squadron commander. "I'm sorry to bother you at home this evening, sir, but Jay Escude insisted I call you." "Congratulations, Spike, Your assignment came in today, you're going to fly Eagles."

Yes! Jay had also received an F-15 assignment. We exchanged high-fives back at my seat and I settled in to watch the movie. My assignment to the F-15 was unique in that it was an inter-command exchange tour. I had volunteered for and had been accepted into the Career Trainer Program.

The idea was that I would stay in the training command and become a flying training specialist. I thoroughly enjoyed teaching and was apparently good at it when I wasn't around! I was told my career would be closely controlled by the training command to include being groomed for command. The biggest drawback I saw was that without major weapons system experience, I'd lack credibility. Nothing says this guy knows what he's talking about than having been out there doing it. The exchange program with Air Combat Command solved that problem but created another. It was *extremely* competitive. Again; God was gracious- not only was I selected for the fighter exchange, but I was selected to fly our newest and most advanced fighter instead of the much older F-111 or the slow and ugly A-10 which were also available in the exchange program.

Sure enough; when I showed up for work on Monday, I had a stack of paperwork which included TDY (temporary duty) orders to attend Lead-in Fighter training (LIFT) at Holloman AFB, NM and additional TDY orders to attend the F-15 FTU (formal training unit) at Tyndall AFB, FL. Finally; I had PCS (permanent change of station) orders to the 48th Fighter Interceptor Squadron at Langley AFB, VA. I read it again; Fighter Interceptor Squadron, *that is so cool!* This changes everything! But first, I had to learn some new things to do with jets besides aerobatics and flying around the country.

CHAPTER IX
LEARNING TO KILL

Soon I was on a lengthy drive to Holloman AFB in Alamogordo, NM. After checking in and settling in at the BOQ; Jay, other LIFT classmates and I went to dinner at a Mexican restaurant on the main drag through Alamogordo. After finishing the best chicken enchilada I've ever eaten; I noticed a woman who looked familiar. I stood up, saying, "Pardon me guys, but I think I know that woman from high school." I walked over to the woman in question and said, "Excuse me but I think we went to high school together, Are you Penny Wrede?" It was, so I joined her and a date who sat quietly while we chatted. It turned out Penny has a gift for Asian languages. In the ten years since FSHS, she was a missionary to Southeast Asia. After Naples, her Air Force father was assigned to Holloman where he retired.

LIFT lasted about two months. The syllabus was flown in T-38s making the program an easier transition for recent UPT graduates. Shirley & Laura flew out for Laura's first birthday.

My chief complaint with LIFT was the IPs. On my first sortie; the IP briefed me on how to fly an overhead pattern. Did he not know I had 2500 IP hours in this airplane? I wasn't a 2Lt fresh out of UPT. I'm the guy who taught that guy's IP how to teach that guy.

My assigned IP had the dangerous habit of making stick inputs from the back seat if the jet wasn't doing exactly what he thought it should be doing. Proper exchange of aircraft control had always been an emphasis item in the training command; especially in the T-38; with its tandem seating, where you couldn't see each other's hands. People have died due to confusion over who was flying the aircraft. So every time my IP touched the stick, I let go, held up my hands, and said, "You have the aircraft," which was proper procedure for transfer of aircraft control. This upset him, so we exchanged few words immediately and some more during the debriefing. My IP flew A-7s for the Puerto Rico Air National Guard. He was a lousy USAF officer role model and his IP skills were unsatisfactory.

Since I was continuing on to the F-15, I flew a syllabus track emphasizing air-to-air maneuvering. As an A-7 pilot, my IP had only recent air-to ground experience. He was a poor choice to be my IP.

Despite his, I finished LIFT as the Top Gun and a distinguished graduate (DG). I then drove home to pack our household goods for shipment to Virginia and load my pick-up for five months in Florida at the F-15 schoolhouse.

I was in a class of five pilots; Jay Escude, along with three recent UPT grads. We were all in the same LIFT class so we were well acquainted as class 86ABT.

The FTU's job was twofold: 1) qualify us as pilots in the single seat F-15A and 2) send us to our gaining units prepared to be good solid wingmen. Academics and emergency procedures training were tough. We learned radar theory to understand how the APG-63 radar and AIM-7 (air intercept missile-7) worked together.

Getting accustomed to a high-G (up to 9 Gs) aircraft was exhausting.

On my initial solo in the easy-to-fly, F-15; I lost all utility hydraulic fluid, which among other things, meant I had no brakes except for the emergency brakes. Rather than rely solely on a back-up system, I used the tail hook to snag a cable stretched across the approach end of the runway to stop after using alternate means to lower the landing gear. Without downside hydraulic pressure I needed my gear pinned and a tow back to the parking ramp. No sense taking any chances with a $63 million jet and my pink body. The end of the story went as described and I arrived back at the parking area after my tow of shame. While I was cheating death in the Florida pan handle; Shirley & Laura were living in my old house on Joffre Drive with Janet who was renting it from my parents. It seemed a great place for my ladies while I was otherwise engaged. After a month's separation, though, I found a condo in Mexico Beach near Tyndall and we reunited in time for Laura to spend her second Christmas on the beach.

I finished the FTU course a couple of months later and we drove up to Virginia in time for Shirley's birthday. She found a nice house for rent in Newport News very close to the church where we met our life-long friends and ski buddies. Fortunately, I was able to check in to my new squadron before I forgot how to fly the Eagle.

CHAPTER X

LIFE WITH ONE SEAT-MAVERICK'S GOT NOTHIN' ON ME

If you treat folks like second class citizens, they will work hard proving they are not. This was the case with the 48th Fighter Interceptor Squadron.

The 48th FIS was an air defense squadron and therefore, looked down on by other F-15 squadrons like those of the 1st Fighter Wing based at Langley. At one time, the air defense mission had its own command, Air Defense Command (ADC). The pilots wore orange flight suits and the jets' tails were painted with colorful designs. (See photo on back cover vs. the tail on my jet in the photo at the end of this chapter.) It took decades for the air defense world to shake this "Cone Head" image.

In the 48th, we unofficially dropped the word "Interceptor" from our designation which differentiated us from other F-15 squadrons. We also replaced our colorful FIS tails with a simple LY for Langley. Finally, we returned to the patch used during WWII when we were the 48th Pursuit Squadron flying P-38 Lightnings.

In those days, "Pursuit" was the designation used for

the "Fighter" we use today. Hence, the sexy fighters of WWII included the P-38, P-40, and the P-51.

Upon arrival at a fighter squadron, new pilots enter Mission Qualification Training. (MQT) This sixty day program lets the squadron observe your skills and train you in the squadron's specific mission and its area of responsibility or AOR. MQT ends with a Mission Ready (MR) check ride; at which point the newbie is declared MR and ready for war.

Dropping the I-word (making the 48FIS into the 48FS) didn't relieve us from our air defense mission. Four small hangars with one jet each, fully fueled and loaded with live weapons, and ready to launch immediately sat across the runways from the squadron.

Between the "barns," as we called them, were the living quarters for two pilots and a maintenance crew. The pilot's lounge contained the largest non- projection TV available and two recliners pushed back just far enough so our feet didn't hit the TV when reclined. We had an impressive collection of VHS tapes. (DVDs were still years away)

The 48FIS alert barns at LangleyAFB

We lounged in our comfortable anti-exposure suit liners and socks. Our anti-exposure suits were inside our flight suits which lay on our beds, unzipped, ready to go. Our G-suits and quick-don flight boots sat nearby.

Our parachute harnesses were already connected to the ejection seat in the aircraft along with our flight publications and gloves. Our helmets with oxygen hose and communications cord already connected sat on the canopy rail. The switches in the cockpit were already positioned for a scramble.

Eagle in a hurry with an AAIM-120,
AMRAAM & ACMI pod

I took my MR check with our weapons and tactics chief, Weapons School grad, J.R. Smith.

An F-15A with 2x AIM-7 Sparrows & a centerline tank

We used two F-14s from NAS Oceana as adversaries. We met them in a warning area (W-72) out over the Atlantic, just east of Virginia Beach. After ensuring everyone was ready to fight, we orbited about twenty five to thirty miles apart. At the "Fight's on" call, we flew south toward the Tomcats as they made a beeline north for us. Our plan was simple. We flew our standard tactical formation; 9 to 12 thousand feet apart, line abreast with a five thousand foot altitude stack (I was higher than JR who was the lead. The F-14s flew much closer to each other in their Vietnam-era fighting wing formation. As we approached the merge, the F-14s were easy to see (it's a big airplane, too.) Plus flying close together like they were; if you saw one, you saw both (that's why JR and I were separated like we were. The Tomcats with all those eyeballs onboard didn't see us until we passed outside their tight formation. They were outflanked. (=not good as you will soon see.) At the merge they turned from the inside out toward us as we expected. This meant that if we turned from the outside in toward them; they'd wind up in front of us both, exposing their hot exhausts, easily absorbing our AIM-9 Sidewinder heat seeking missiles in a matter of seconds.

With four jets turning within three miles of each other, it's critical everyone sees each other and knows who's fighting who. For JR and me, I initiated the conversation as briefed by saying, "Pinto two, tally two, visual." Tally two means I see both bad guys. Visual means I see my, lead. JR responded with switch! That meant I was to engage his bandit while he engaged mine.

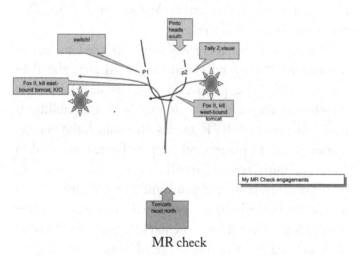

MR check

Because of the geometry described earlier, we both were in position for immediate shots.

"Pinto two, fox two (heat seeking missile fired) kill the eastbound Tomcat." Pinto one, fox two kill the west bound Tomcat, Knock it off. Pinto one knock it off. "Pinto two knock it off." Everyone is required to acknowledge the knock it off call, even the pilot who initiates it. (It sounds goofy but that's the rule.) The deceased F-14s acknowledged their demise and limped back south to set up for another engagement. After a fuel check and reset to our starting points JR called Fight's on again and we went looking for more Tomcats to spank.

The second engagement was a repeat of the first as was the third. Three engagements, six kills, zero losses. This was fun! I passed the check ride and became MR.

We routinely spanked the F-14s like this. They always wanted to "turn and burn" even though they were at a distinct disadvantage against the F-15. They continually requested scenarios that lead to close-in visual fights. This was great fun but lousy training.

These very expensive jets were designed to launch missiles BVR (beyond visual range). In fact, the F-14 coupled with its expensive ($1 million each) Phoenix missile was one of the first to exploit this capability. If executed properly, BVR tactics eliminated the merge, reducing risk to planes and people. There's no need to "turn and burn" with a fireball.

Our attitude was; if you want to turn with us, you must earn that right by surviving to the merge. Pre-merge missile defense was a fundamental for us. But the Tomcats from Oceana seemed to be annoyed by it.

To be fair; those guys required a lot training time to operate off ships. (Read: moving postage stamp-size airfields) Thank God, they are gutsy enough to do it. I prefer my 9000' x 300' landlocked runway with an extra 1000' on each end thrown in, just in case.

But when it comes time to go beak to beak with a MiG that's shooting back, I'd bet on the Eagle Driver in an F-15 every time. Sitting alert was boring but it allowed ample time to work on other things. I earned my Master of Aeronautical Science degree while at Langley.

We always kept a radio tuned to the military guard frequency as well as the airspace monitor for the mid-Atlantic coast. If we ever heard the radio call beginning with, "unknown rider- unknown rider" we climbed into our flight gear in case the scramble horn went off. If anything needed to be checked out, Giant Killer (radar facility monitoring our airspace off the east coast of the Mid-Atlantic States sounded the horn. At night, the overhead lights switched to red. We stopped whatever we were doing, got into our flight gear, and ran downstairs to enter the barns. In the ADC, orange flight suit, days some facilities had poles to slide down like firemen. Once downstairs, we ran into the barn, over to the ladder, climbed up, and stepped into the cockpit. The crew chief was at the plane already holding the right shoulder strap of our harnesses up to make getting into them faster. As we reached through the shoulder strap we pulled a handle which began the engine start sequence.

Once the generators started supplying electrical power to the jet (the Eagle was designed without a battery.), we began throwing switches and checking systems in a rapid but orderly fashion and finished strapping in. Our goal was; horn to airborne in five minutes or less.

Once the radio functioned, the wingman, transmitted, "Mike Golf two's up" on the auxiliary radio. The flight lead then used the main radio, "Langley tower, Mike Golf's standing by for words. Tower read the clearance and authenticated us to make sure everyone on frequency was legit. By now the crew chiefs had pulled the protective seeker head covers off the missiles and the many remove before flight pins with red streamers on the aircraft. Then they stood by and waited for our hand- signal to pull the wheel chawks, which came quickly. Tower, Mike Golf's rolling. Mike Golf, Langley Tower, you are cleared for take-off, runway zero eight, winds, zero seven zero at fifteen, the altimeter is three zero one three. Three zero one three, Mike Golf. Using the high-speed taxi way, Mike Golf one rolled onto the active runway, lined up on the downwind side, selected full afterburner, and became airborne in a matter of seconds. Mike Golf two copied his leader except delaying the takeoff roll on the upwind side slightly taking care not to stare at the five stages of afterburner flame exiting MG01's nozzles. MG02 soon followed his leader's flashing lights into the night sky. Neither knew why they were being scrambled. Would they return with all their missiles or was this just an AFE or Alert Force Evaluation?

Mike Golf, contact departure, channel four. Mike Golf, go channel four. Two. (Pronounced toop) Using only his radar (and an occasional peek out the front window), MG02 remains two miles in trail of MG01. Both pilots adjust their interior lights as dimly as possible while still illuminating the instruments adequately. On clear nights with a bright moon, many interior lights could be turned off.

Now that adrenaline rush of the scramble is over, it's time to take a breath, relax, take a look around outside and do some house keeping by arranging any approach books you might need later. Then, take a look at the moon, the stars, and any city lights which might be visible and try to identify them. Distances can be deceiving at night. What you think is DC might actually be Richmond. For the most part, we left the lights of the Hampton Roads cities behind us and steered east out over the dark Atlantic. On the way out, I played the "what if" game. What if my left engine fell off right now; where would I go? What's the closest emergency divert field? How do I find out? Can I see it from here? Would I need to pull out an aeronautical chart? Is that kind of information in the 48th Fighter Squadron Pilot Aid? Let's check. Where's my flashlight? The Soviet, TU-95 Bear bomber patrolled our east coast during the Cold War. They were our most often intercepted intruder.(See back cover) It was way cool to fly up close to that shiny silver plane with the big red star on its tail and wave to the tail-gunner in the back and the flight crew in the cockpit. Sometimes, the tail gunner took videos of us. We had pistol grip – mounted auto focus 35 mm cameras to take their pictures, too. Rather than tail numbers like us, the Soviets put their aircraft numbers on the nose wheel door. I suppose this made them easy to see with the bomber parked on the ramp. Flying up under the Bear's nose to photo graph that nose wheel door was sometimes dicey. They knew this and would steer for clouds or use their radar altimeters to fly very close to the water. Stormin Seip and I were trailing two Bears in bad weather one night. We were each locked up on one following them from about 9000 feet back. They descended low over the water and began to weave back and forth in what could have only been an attempt to have us run into each other. If this is a "Cold War," why am I sweating?

WILLY TELL

William Tell is a huge biennial air-to-air competition hosted by Tyndall AFB. Fighter Wings from all over North America spend months preparing their entrants(pilots and planes) for the canned air-to- air scenarios They send their best pilots(having had months of WT-specific training) wearing custom-tailored flight suits and aircraft that were tweaked and pampered for months. They sported fresh paint jobs. It's a real dog 'n pony show and a huge waste of time and money. The adversary tactics were known and the competitors were well-practiced against them.

LONG ARROW

The annual Long Arrow competition is very different. Pilots don't know they're competing until twenty-four hours before the event. At that time, one of four letters (A through D) is drawn from a hat. If the letter drawn is a B, Then the competing squadron's B Flight competes with five jets that are already on that day's schedule (four to compete plus one airborne spare). The flight commander must lead the 4 ship and flight lead qualified pilots cannot fly as wingmen in positions two and four. The four plus spare rendezvous with a tanker, cycle everyone across the boom to ensure all could take fuel. This was the only reason the spare could be used. The routing from the home base to the unknown competition airspace had to be at least one thousand miles at which time the competing team topped off their tanks, entered the competition airspace and fought an unknown number and type of adversary aircraft; flying whatever tactic they chose to either defeat or get past the four F-15s they knew they would face. That was it. No ringer, practiced pilots, no aircraft that had been babied for the last three months, no fresh paint, no Gucci flight suits, no canned scenarios; just five pilots flying only the positions for which they were qualified. There was no way to prepare ahead of time for Long Arrow, except to have the whole squadron trained to excel all the time. The 48th Fighter Squadron was not invited to compete in Long Arrow I. Pick your reason: a) We an air defense unit flying around with two jets intercepting stuff, b) We flew old A-models and didn't stand a chance against the newer C-model squadrons, or c) We weren't trained well enough in four-ship tactics to be competitive. *ALL WRONG*. Tell someone they aren't good enough and standby to be amazed. B Flight of the 48th Fighter Squadron *won* Long Arrow II. When Long Arrow III came around, A Flight was drawn from the hat. *Guess who was in A Flight.* You guessed it! I was a relatively new, 2-ship flight lead. I was chosen as the airborne spare. I could substitute for anyone except the 4-ship lead; Flight commander, Major "Whip" Biederman. 1Lt. Sammy "Pitch" Black was two, Captain Rick "Mobile" Holmes was three, and Captain Maurice "Shamu" Salcedo (former T-38 FAIP) was four. After a pancake breakfast in the squadron, the five of us took off to meet our tanker, a KC-135(Boeing 707 converted into a flying gas station) the join up went smoothly. Cycling across the boom was normal except Mobile (#3) couldn't open his air refueling

door. Whip quickly decided to put me in as number three
so Mobile could return home before burning too much
fuel heading west away from Langley. With Mobile gone,
I took a sip ensuring my jet was good to go. It was, so I
took my position on the wing of the tanker opposite Whip
and Shamu moved over to my wing. There, all set to cruise
a while and look out the window. We were already west
of the Appalachian Mountains. A while later, we hung
a left around St. Louis (Home of McDonnell-Douglas
where our planes were built). We then headed southeast
and gradually the Gulf coast came into view. Someone
said on the aux radio, "Looks like we're headed to Tyndall
or Eglin airspace." We were loaded with ACMI pods on
one of our four heat seeking missile rails so I said, "With
these ACMI pods, I'm thinking, Tyndall's ACMI range."
(Over the Gulf of Mexico).

ACMI stands for Air Combat Maneuvering
Instrumentation. The pods we carried on one of our
four wing pylon missile rails tapped into our flight and
weapons computers transmitting data to buoys on the
water below. This data was then transferred to a room
at Tyndall were it was converted to avatars accurately
depicting the fight on a large video screen. In TOP GUN
this system was visible when Charlie critiqued Maverick's
Split S as being too aggressive and someone says, that's
the gutsiest move I ever saw, man. Maverick responded
to Charlie's critique with some fighter pilot talk about
reversing on a hard cross and going to guns quicker. What
he said sounded cool and all, especially since he used his
hands but what he said actually made no sense. We were
all familiar with Tyndall's airspace and the fuel required

for recovering from the ACMI range, so Whip quickly established a bingo fuel.

"Bingo" is the fuel state that requires maneuvering to stop and the aircraft to recover to base and land without receiving traffic priority. When anyone declares "Bingo," a "knock it off" follows immediately and the fight is over.

In the F-15, the fuel gage has a little index pointer that rotates around the fuel gage and can beset to the desired bingo fuel. If the index is set, a female voice declares "Bingo fuel" when the fuel level pointer reaches the index. "Betty" (the voice warning system), sounds off if something bad happens such as an over-G, engine overheat or fire.

With our bingo established, we topped off our tanks before establishing our assigned CAP (combat air patrol) position. Whip but us in a tactical wall formation: 9 to 12 thousand feet spacing, line abreast with altitude stacks. In this formation we fenced-in. (Set the cockpit switches for the fight) We also performed a five to six G, G-awareness turn to warm our bodies up.

Satisfied our jets and our bodies were ready for the fight, we checked in with a weapons controller onboard the AWACS (Airborne Warning and control system) – call sign: Magic. We each searched our assigned piece of the sky for bogeys. A bogey is an unknown radar contact. When identified (in accordance with established Rules of Engagement, as a hostile, he becomes a bandit. For this fight; if it's not an F-15, it's a bandit. (It can't get much easier than that.).

Based on Magic's call, we refined our search. There appeared to be two groups shaping up in the southeast end of the range. As soon as they flew past the bulls-eye(a common reference point from which we positioned ourselves or the enemy), they 1 would meet our commit criteria and we would leave the CAP orbit and fly straight at the bogies accelerating to above the Mach. Whip radioed, "Commit, commit." Letting AWACS know we were leaving the CAP. We didn't know it but we also let an audience gathered in the ACMI facility know what we were doing. The audience included referees and our operations officer; Lt Col Bill "Frito" Lay. As we closed on the bogies there were definitely two groups. In a lead-trail formation with the trailers about five miles behind the leaders. The lead group looked a little heavy. (More than one airplane) It was time for one last look to sanitize the extremes (very high & very low) to check for any one we might have missed before we "melded" our radar search areas so we all saw the same radar picture before the targeting shooting started. After searching in the weeds one last time, I melded. Still two groups, lead-trail, heavy leaders. Whip called out, Devil one (nice call sign, huh?) two groups, lead-trail, five mile split east bulls-eye ten, multiple leaders. Two same, three same, four same, Magic, same. High fives all around, we've got this doped. Moments later the lead group began splitting. Our sort plan called for one and two to take the leaders while three (me) and four (Shamu) took the trailers who were also looking heavy now. Devil three, leaders splitting, trailers heavy. Four same. Magic same. By now the leaders had split enough that it was obvious that they were trying to outflank us. This was a classic Soviet tactic – distract us with the leaders, while the trailer blew through at high speed. Pay attention to the trailers and the leaders outflank you and spank you.

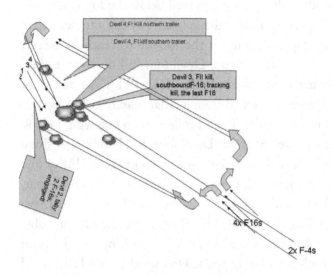

Devil 4 Fl Kill northern trailer

Devil 4, Fl kill southern trailer

Devil 3, Fll kill, southboundF-16; tracking kill, the last F16

Devil 2, tally 2 F-16s engaged

4x F16s

2x F-4s

Long Arrow III

Whip said, "Devil one sorted northern leader." Devil two sorted southern leader. Devil three, standby. I hated interrupting the rhythm of our communications but I needed a little more time to see what the trailers were up to. There, they are spreading out, too, but not aggressively like their leaders. Devil three, trailers splitting. Four same. Magic same. Devil three, sorted southern trailer. Devil four sorted northern trailer. Devil two, tally two F-16s southern leaders engaged! Calm down, Pitch; go kill 'em, I thought. I told Shamu, "Head's up four northern leaders may be the same".

Whip who was to my right (south) leaned right to help out Pitch who just found himself outnumbered. As Whip distanced himself from me, I climbed so that I could look through Whip toward Pitch and the Vipers further to the south. This put Shamu well below me to my left. He called, fox one (radar missile fired) northern trailer. After the appropriate time for the missile to reach its target, Shamu drew first blood. Devil four kill northern trailer. But what about the northern leaders I suspected were two F-16s? I switched from a radar search to looking out the window, again. Then I rolled up on one wing to look down. There's Shamu. "Devil four, F-4 bandit nose three miles." Devil four contact (radar lock) there, Talley one F-4, fox one (. Moments later, Shamu said, Devil four, kill F-4 westbound F-4, six thousand. So we had two F-4 strikers(both killed by Shamu) escorted by probably four F-16s Whip and Pitch were working two F-*16s* in the south but what happened to the other two I suspected were up north with Shamu and me? They *had* to be close by now. This didn't feel right. I was missing something. It's time for another quick look outside.

There's Shamu right where he should be. Uh-oh, "Devil four, break right F-16 bandit your six, one mile!" Shamu started an impressive break turn but it was too late. Devil four; you're dead declared a referee on the fight frequency. Devil four, Shamu acknowledged. Doggone it! I yelled in my mask as I pounded my fist on the canopy rail. That was my fault! I should have done a better visual lookout! Maybe I didn't roll the elevation wheel with my left pinky far enough down so that I wasn't picking the F-16s up on radar. I'll figure out my mistake when we review our tapes. It's too bad these A-models don't have flare dispensers to counter the heat seeking missiles. At least Shamu killed the strikers the F-16s were supposed to protect, I thought. But now was no time for regrets or excuses.

Now was time to get my head back in the fight which wasn't over. As I called for Shamu's break turn, I rolled inverted and pulled my nose onto the F-16s. So now I was pointed straight down at the Gulf with two bandits happily flying south over the beautiful water. I needed to change that. The noontime sun was high overhead at my six so they didn't see me descend from the heavens behind them. They were line abreast about a mile apart at seven thousand feet headed toward their buddies who were wrapped up with Whip and Pitch. Make that *buddy*. Whip had killed one of the southern F-16s. I needed to dispatch these guys before they became a threat to Whip or Pitch. I didn't use my radar because I didn't want their fuzz busters (Radar Warning Receivers) to give away my presence. Instead I used my left index finger to bore sight my sidewinder seeker head. Now the seeker head was looking wherever I pointed the jet. I used the HUD symbology to aim the missile at one of the bandits. I heard a good tone in my headset, so I uncaged the missile's seeker head with my right ring finger to ensure it tracked my intended victim. (Required for a valid, single – shot kill.) The higher pitched tone in my headset told me it was, so I pressed the pickle button with my right thumb to "launch" the AIM-9M training missile I carried.

Our training missiles were the real thing with the warhead and rocket motor removed. The plane didn't know the difference so the pilot received the same HUD symbology and seeker head tones that he would with a live missile. Thanks to the Eagle's design, I was able to do all this without having to take my hands off the stick and throttles. We called this playing the piccolo. "Devil three, fox two kill the western F-16, south bound at seven thousand." In the ACMI facility, the audience saw a tiny little missile depart my avatar and track over to the bandit's avatar. Upon arrival a coffin appeared on the F-16 avatar. The morted F-16 rocked his wings to acknowledge his being taken out of the fight. His wing man took this opportunity to defend himself and made a break turn. I pressed the attack to avenge Shamu.

"Devil three's engaged with one F-16 west bulls-eye, ten." This call let Whip and Pitch know what was going on so they could help me kill this pesky adversary if they were in the vicinity and had nothing better to do.

The F-16 is no slouch in a knife fight like the F-14. Its great thrust-to-weight ratio lets it turn on an aeronautical dime, but its slow-speed handling suffers because of its tiny little wings. The F-16 community often criticized the Eagle for its size. They called it a flying tennis court. Because the F-16 has only one engine; when it fails, gravity rules. Fighters make lousy gliders. This happened so often in the early years of the F-16 that the rest of the Air Force took to calling it the Lawn Dart.

In truth, the F-15 is so large because of the requirement to push a 36-inch radar antenna at 2.5 mach. This required a huge nose cone which drove the need for two engines; which provides the Eagle with more thrust than the airplane weights. The F-15's size means the flying tennis court handles very well at slow speeds and high altitude. Now, back to the fight:

I kept the pressure on this little gomer to keep him turning and depleting his energy. Apparently, he didn't like my big airplane so close, pointing at him all the time so he tried staking it up in the vertical. Big mistake dude. You don't have the energy for this, I thought as I kept the pressure just as high going uphill with him. Let's try going downhill; the gomer must have thought, because that's what he did. But he did it gradually. This guy was doing little to keep me out of his map case. His gradual descent allowed him to increase his airspeed enough to go vertical again, so up he went. But now he's in a quandary, what next? As he approached the apex of his climb, with airspeed bleeding away, he had little choice but to descend again. Has he never heard the adage, "Beware the Eagle on its back?" When inverted an aircraft pulling eight Gs gets the turning performance of nine Gs due to the addition of earth's gravity. Many pilots call this God's G. Oh well, I'll show him.

I followed him up and immediately noticed my excessive closure because my airspeed was still quite high and his was gone; as he pulled through over the top, as if flying aerobatics instead of fighting for his life. I rolled on my back, centered the stick, and then buried it in my lap while tensing every muscle between my navel and toes against my G- suit which had inflated rock-hard to give me something to push my muscles against. This anti-G straining maneuver (AGSM) prevents blood from pooling in my lower extremities and forces some back up to my head. Failure to perform a good AGSM results in oxygen deprivation in the head leading to tunnel vision, loss of vision or unconsciousness; all of which are bad when flying. (On a scale from good to bad)

My jet turned as if on a hinge. My nose was now pointed down inside the bandit's turn circle and I was accelerating. The F-16 tried going vertical again but this time as before, he was going uphill fast; losing energy. With my excellent energy state, I could make a tight, high- G turn inside his turn circle and still go vertical him.

He must have been impressed with my last-turn, because it looked like he was going to try one. Only, when he rolled on his back, I was right there still trying to "get close to my work." To quote 48 FS commander George "Boof" Booth, the best BFMer I ever saw. I selected the gun with my left thumb. (I was too close for a sidewinder). The HUD symbology changed to display the gun reticle as the radar automatically locked on.

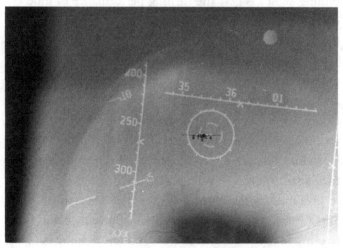

The F-15A gun reticle

My range was *almost* perfect (I might have been a tad close.); I had a perfect plan form view of the F-16, more grace! I could see the pilot's dark visor as he turned his head to watch me kill him. Why aren't you jinking, guy?

A jink is a last-ditch maneuver to move your jet out of the stream of bullets that are headed your way shortly. An effective jink requires good energy. This bandit was unable to jink because his energy was gone He wasn't even trying to jink. His control surfaces weren't moving at all. He might have just given up and relaxed from the high-G fight. (I doubt this was the case; giving up is not in a fighter pilot's DNA). I knew he hadn't had a GLOC (G-induced Loss of Consciousness) because I saw him move his head.

After a minor adjustment to put the tiny pipper on the pilot's cranium, I squeezed the trigger for about a second and a half; enough to put roughly 150 rounds of 20 millimeter, high explosive incendiary (HEI) through his cockpit. A split second later, a little triangle appeared in the reticle on the Viper's canopy. This was the RTR (pronounced ratter) or rounds at target range. If this had been real, the RTR shows were the bullets would hit the target. According to our training rules, if the RTR touches the fuselage, it's a valid shot for a kill.

These 20 millimeter rounds don't just punch holes in the target; they explode on contact, like small artillery shells. One round of 20mm HEI would have ruined this guy's day. But 150 rounds through the canopy would have separated the cockpit from the rest of the plane and not left much of the pilot for the fish. The plane wreckage would make a nice artificial reef, though. "Devil three, tracking kill the last F-16." That was a gutsy call. My situational awareness told me all four F-16s had been defeated. I got two of them. Whip and Pitch spanked their southern bandits. I hope we didn't miss somebody. With all the adversaries dead and our fuel running low, Betty would be calling soon. Whip knocked off the fight. We reformed and flew back to Tyndall feeling good about our six kills. But I didn't feel like celebrating just yet. I lost my wingman.

Knowing we would be watched, we went into air show mode - we took extra care to be in perfect position as Whip led us up initial in close echelon formation. Once over the approach end of the runway, Whip pitched out crisply. We each mimicked his pitchout at five second intervals. This gave us the required spacing to allow all four of us to land on the same runway, alternating sides for our touchdowns. We each slowed during the pitch to get below the flap limit speed of 250 knots; then we each lowered our gear and flaps while maintaining our spacing. As we rolled off the perch in sequence, and reported, "Devil #, gear down, full stop." Devils, you're cleared to land.

At the end of the runway, we parked briefly in the dearming area to have our gear pins installed. After, we made the long taxi back to the parking area in formation, still wanting to look like the professional team we were. We parked side by side; shut down our engines simultaneously on Whips command, and opened our canopies in sequence.

I was anxious to deplane. The flight had been over seven hours long and I needed to use the restroom -now. Our arrival was taped by a local Panama City news channel. After I climbed down the ladder, a female reporter stuck a microphone in my face and asked about the mission. I very briefly told her about how strenuous the fight had been. Then she asked if I learned anything. "Yes ma'am," I said, "I don't have a seven point three- hour bladder. I need to be excused. And I walked inside for some very welcome relief.

That evening, Tyndall hosted a huge party at the O' Club for all the competitors to announce the winners. The tension built as they announced the team results, finally, came time to present the Top Team award that everyone was there to win. They announced, "With six kills and *zero* losses," (Dang, I though, it can't be us, we lost one because of me!) the Long Arrow III Top Team is the 48th Fighter Squadron from Langley AFB, Virginia!! It turned out the shot taking out Shamu was invalid so the kill didn't count! (His impressive break turn might have put him inside the minimum range for the AIM-9. If the F-16 pilot shot from inside min range, the shot would be adjudicated not valid). The whole place was on their feet clapping and cheering for us. *This was incredible!* Grace at a knife-fight in a phone booth with two vipers – Who'd have thunk? The 48th FIS with our old A models and cone head air defense mission had back-to-back Long Arrow victories! Frito had a huge smile as he shook each hand. "Spike, you gunned that last guy shooting straight up while he was inverted. It was a thing of beauty on the ACMI." "Thanks, sir, it was more fun that way."

The evening news carried our story but edited out my last comment about needing the restroom. Each of us was presented with beautiful, replica 1861 Navy Colt black powder revolvers in cherry display boxes. I had an oak shadow box built for mine so it matched our furnishings better (Shirley's input). The next day Whip requested clearance to taxi with, "Tyndall ground, Devil zero one request taxi for four Long Arrow Champions. We taxied and took off and cruised back to Langley in a little over an hour. We tried to look even more impressive flying up initial, landing, and parking than we did at Tyndall. The whole squadron plus our families were there to welcome us home. A huge sign reading "Standard!" hung on the squadron building. We had a hug- fest after we climbed down our ladders. A base newspaper photographer took a picture of the four of us with our revolvers tucked into our G-suits. As I type, that same revolver is proudly displayed on my bookcase, three feet to my right. I won Top Gun twice while in the 48th and once later in the 59th but the Long Arrow victory was the highlight of my flying career.

My F-15A, 76104 drew a crowd at Langley's 1988 Open House]

CHAPTER XI

HANGING UP THE G-SUIT

The phone rang in the alert facility while I was sitting alert approaching the end of my three-year tour with the 48th. It was the fighter assignments manager at the AF Personnel Center (AFPC). Hey Bill, (You've got the wrong guy, buddy, nobody calls me Bill.) I've got an assignment here with your name on it. Gulp. "Oh yeah? What's it say?" It's what we call a two plus three; you do two years as an ALO (Air Liaison Officer) with the Army in Grafenweir, Germany followed by a guaranteed three- year tour flying Eagles again at Bitburg. (Also in Germany) "Can I talk to my wife and get back to you?" Sure, call me back tomorrow. To avoid any prejudice, I kept my career trainer status to myself with the exception of my first flight commander, Major "Stormin" Seip (now a major general). After talking with AFPC, I called Stormin'. He advised me to talk to Frito, which I did. Frito was surprised to learn of my career trainer status and said, you know, Spike, *we might want to keep you.* This was music to my ears. I called AFPC and told him what my Ops Officer said. "Any chance I stay in the Eagle?" No way, he said. If word got out that our exchange tour guys didn't come back, we'd have to shut down the program. "Okay, what now?" I could really use you as a T-37 IP at

Sheppard (Wichita Falls, Texas). "So I just spent three very successful years as an F-15 pilot and now you want me to fly the Tweet?"

Yeah, we want you career Trainer guys to fly both airplanes (T-37 and T-38). That way, when you're being looked at for squadron command, you can go either way. "What if I opt out of the Tweet and take my chances on the command thing; can I stay in the Eagle?" Nope. Within a week I had orders to the 89th FTS at Sheppard AFB, TX. *God is in control.* We loved living here in Virginia. *God has a plan.* We loved our church in Newport News and our very close Sunday school class which included best friends and ski buddies, Rob and Kathy Farmer and the Elliots (Jim and Anita) *God is in control.*

Church gang on a ski trip at Snowshoe, WV 1989

Leaving these people was the toughest departure I had in twelve moves. After our moving van pulled away, we drove over to the Farmer's home for our last night in Virginia for the next fifteen years. We left early the next morning for our long drive to Texas. Fortunately, the FTW at Sheppard conducted their PIT in-house, so I didn't need to go through the program again in San Antonio. Flying the painfully slow, underpowered, and delightfully loud T-37 after the F-15 took getting used to, but I got through PIT without difficulty.

Wichita Falls was a hot, dusty city. The falls were manmade and turned off when they rolled up the sidewalks at night. The flight to which I was assigned was commanded by a British squadron leader. I was appointed his assistant flight commander. We had several IPs from different NATO countries. What's with all these foreigners?

The FTW at Sheppard hosts ENJJPTP, (Euro-NATO Joint Jet Pilot Training Program). NATO member nations without their own pilot training programs sent their students to Sheppard. Almost all of the students went back to their countries to fly fighters so the syllabus was more fighter-oriented than UPT and fighter pilots were required as IPs, even in Tweets – Hence, my presence. I found many of the NATO IPs especially the Danes and Dutch had great flying skills but disgraceful airmanship.

I had a German student (2Lt. Schumacher) who kept me on my toes. With his photographic memory, he soon, knew the books as well as any IP in the wing. He was the only student to ever unfold and study the electrical system wiring diagram in the Dash one (the book detailing the systems and procedures for an aircraft.) He discovered a particular component required X volts. (Where X < 12) He also knew the battery and generators supplied twelve volts. He found one step-down transformer but it wouldn't suffice to reduce the voltage to X for the component in question. Sir, there must be a further voltage reduction but it's not in the diagram. (Read with a German accent.) Good catch Lt. Schumacher, Let's check it out. We went to the electrical shop in maintenance. He's right, sir. There is another voltage step down but your diagram doesn't show it. Lt Schumacher was built like Arnold Swartzenegger, too. He probably returned to Germany to fly the MiG-29 Fulcrums the GAF inherited after German Reunification.

I'm sure he's had an excellent career. While at Sheppard; Desert Storm came and went. Shirley and I just finished walking in the mall. We learned of the war's start on the car radio in the parking lot. We immediately prayed for my USAF brethren in harm's way that evening. I stayed up watching the war on CNN until the first wave of two thousand sorties returned. Everyone came home that first night! If Saddam Hussein was looking for a holy war, he got one, because flying that many sorties into the most heavily defended city since Hanoi with no losses was no less a miracle of God than His parting the Red Sea. One hundred days later it was over. Our ground troops supported by coalition air forces seriously spanked Iraq. Shortly after the war, Shirley's mother, Jean, was diagnosed with cancer. *God is in control.* The Air Force transfers members for humanitarian reasons. I requested a humanitarian move to get us closer to Orange Park, FL where Shirley's parents lived. I was hopeful AFPC would find me a flying job either as an adviser to the Florida Air

National Guard in Jax or teaching at Tyndall which is only five hours away. AFPC elected to send me to Fort Stewart, Georgia as an Air Liaison Officer (ALO) to the 24th Infantry Division (Mechanized) commanded by future Drug Czar, Maj Gen Barry McCaffrey. Ft Stewart is in Hinesville, Georgia near Savannah, only two hours from Orange Park. We found a nice home to rent in Richmond Hill, a thirty minute drive from my ALO detachment.

Officially, we were Detachment 2, 507th Air Control Wing. As soon as I checked in; I left to learn the ALO business at AGOS, the Air-Ground Operations School at Hurlburt Field in Ft Walton Beach, FL from where I would retire fourteen years in the future. I returned home after a few short weeks as a DG. What I didn't learn at AGOS, I picked up quickly at Ft. Stewart – The Army seriously lacks a sense of humor.

Desert Storm was so recent that when I showed up; much of the division's equipment was still in transit back from the desert, as was our little fifty-man detachment's equipment; Primarily HMMWVs (highly maneuverable multi-wheeled vehicles with a large rack full of radios (GRC-206)(HF, VHF, UHF, FM, you name it.) When we unpacked our computers, sand poured out of them but they worked fine. Our function as ALOs boiled down to Advise, Assist, and if necessary - Control. We had enlisted air controllers who were qualified to put eyes on target and control the aircraft attacking them. But we ALOs were also qualified to provide terminal control. Because we would be exposed to hostile fire, we carried side arms and assault rifles. We primarily worked at the brigade and division levels to integrate air power into the ground scheme of maneuver. We often reminded commanders how the system worked. Just because you want it, doesn't mean you'll get it. Army commanders are used to getting their way, so when a request for air support was not approved we reminded them it was likely disapproved by a green-suiter, not a blue-suiter. (Don't shoot the messenger.) I always kept a diagram of the air request process on hand for this. The Air Tasking Order (ATO) is the large document tasking all air units. It specifies the number and type of aircraft and the ordinance they were to carry to strike a specific target, sometimes specifying where to place the weapon on the target. It dictated pre- or post-strike refueling and routing to get through friendly forced without getting shot. Something this complex takes 72 hours to prepare. Asking the Army to know what specific air support they want three days out was often a showstopper; and we got beat up quite a bit for it.

Sometimes the Army commander doesn't know what he's asking. During one exercise, a brigade commander wanted USAF EF-111s to support apache helicopters he was sending down range. The EF-111 is a low density, high demand asset. Everyone wants jammers but we don't have many. Plus, they are a very fast aircraft; not the best choice to jam for helicopters.

Captain RD Shanks, was the 2nd brigade ALO with this demanding brigade commander who really, really wanted those EF-111s. When RD told him they were not available; the Army Colonel, who knew enough to be *challenging* (I changed that last word from dangerous); asked, about Prowlers. The Navy's EA-6B Prowler is a carrier-based jammer. RD, wanting to show he knew a thing or two, countered, I can check sir, but a lot will depend on the carrier's cycle time. We'd have to be real lucky to match up with the carrier's cycle time. The Colonel, knowing RD had control of all those radios I mentioned said; Get the CAG (Carrier Air Group) on the radio. The CAG is the man on the carrier responsible for all flight operations. Now RD was stuck. Our Det simulated most C2 (command and control) nodes for air operations but we didn't have someone pretending to be the CAG; a force provider, not a C2 node. We never did. - because brigade commanders just don't talk to CAGs. What the colonel asked was highly unusual. RD, an F-4 weapons systems officer (WSO) stalled the best he could but the colonel was tenacious, continuing to press RD until RD couldn't take it anymore. "Look, sir, this is just an exercise. There is no carrier, there is no CAG." "You can talk to the JFACC if you want, but you'd be talking to airman Snuffy back at the det." The JFACC or Joint Force Air Component Commander is the USAF general in command of all air assets in the war.

Get out of my TOC (tactical operations center). "Yes sir." Before he left; RD called me at the division TOC. Spike, I got kicked out of the TOC. "Okay, what happened?" He explained. I had worked with this particular brigade commander and the story sounded right.

RD, how about you work up here at division and I'll take your place at 2nd brigade. Deal. We disclosed our positions and swapped jobs. I apologized for RD's behavior and made nice with the Colonel. I told him I'd try a work around to get him the EW (electronic warfare) support he wanted. RD was very competent but he let his frustration get the best of him occasionally.

Sometime during my ALO tour, RD and I left the Det to meet with one of the brigades in the field. We radioed our guys to get their exact location. RD drove. On the way, I realized that we had forgotten to get the sign/countersign (sort of like a password) to be allowed inside the wire at the TOC we were visiting. No problem, RD said. I got this. Great, I thought, apparently RD remembered to get the countersign. We pulled up to the entry control point at the TOC and an MP came up to RD's window and gave him the sign to which RD should have responded with the countersign. Instead RD responded with, "We don't know about all that stuff, we're with the band."

Maybe the MP was confused by our Air Force insignia and the fact that an officer was driving the hummer. In the Army, officers have enlisted drivers take them everywhere. Seeing an officer behind the wheel was unusual. Or maybe he had just had a long day; but the MP waved us through! "You got this, RD? That was your plan?!" "We're with the band?" We're in aren't we? Many times we were challenged with culture clashes. The Army and the Air Force were very different.

Prior to a major deployment to Fort Irwin's National training Center (NTC) in the Desert near Barstow, California; a battalion commander was out of sorts because our Hummers were not painted with his battalion markings. He wasn't going to let them on the train with his battalion equipment for the ride to NTC. My guys called me so I called the battalion commander and he told me that our equipment couldn't go until they were painted. "That's fine with me, sir. We'll just bring them back to the Det, park them in our yard and my guys can take some leave while you're at NTC with no one to control your CAS" (close air support).

"Sir, our HMMWVs are painted in accordance with Air Force directives. You have no more authority to require them painted than you do to require an A-10 or a C-5 painted." They go as is or they don't go but *I will not violate Air Force directives* and paint them. He backed down and accepted our Hummers and the CAS they provided. While at Det 2, I completed Air Command and Staff College by correspondence. This helped with my promotion to Major. Now where do I go from here?

The Air Force was in the middle of a RIF (reduction in force) when my two years at Fort Stewart were coming to an end. Before pilots in non-flying billets (like me) returned to a cockpit, they needed to meet a return to fly (RTF) board. This was new. It was kind of like a promotion board for pilots only. It was all about the math. There were more pilots needing assignments than empty cockpits so they wanted folks with promotion potential and came up with this RTF board idea.

One AFPC officer I talked to told me I should look for a cushy staff job somewhere nice and hang on until I reached twenty years and retire. Finish the last eight years of my career in a staff job? No Thank you. Thank God (who else?) I was selected by the RTF board which meant I was cockpit-worthy. But I didn't know what cockpit or where. All AFPC told me was they had a list of available planes and a list of pilots to plug into them. They were working it and he'd call me later as the lists got smaller. "Are there any Eagles on the list?" Yes, we've got a little of everything on the list. I called weekly to check the list. On one call he said, I've got an F-111 to Canon (NM) or and OA-10(airborne forward air controller) to Korea (one year, family stays in the states) I can give you right now if you want them. No thanks. Shirley's mother had passed away a month or two before so it would not be a good time for me to leave the continent and I figured it was a little late for me to learn the air-to-ground business of the F-111; although a fellow ALO, who had flown F-4s before the F-15 assured me that if you can fly the F-15, you can fly anything. After a while, the good news came: *I was to return to theF-15!* More Grace? You be the judge.

AFPC told me I must have blown them away at the RTF board because they were looking at either sending me to 1 FW at Langley, or 33 FW at Eglin, or 32 FS at Soesterburg AB in the Netherlands, or a guard advisor at Otis ANGB (air national guard base) on Cape Cod (which sounded just as foreign as Holland); it looks like someone wants you back in the Eagle. (*Hmm, I wonder who.*) "I haven't been overseas yet so the 32 FS gig sounds perfect." Great, we'll contact these units and see if they want you. "What if nobody wants me?"

'Let's not worry about that right now. "OK, but make sure you let me know when it's time to worry."

One of my favorite verses in the Bible fits most situations in life. In Psalms 46:10 God says: Be still and know that I am God. Okay, Lord, *You're in control* and *you've got the plan. You've got this.*

Shirley and I could get excited about any of the locations being discussed and I was certainly excited about flying the Eagle again. Not so fast, Jonesy…

CHAPTER XII
EAGLES AT THE BEACH

Time marched on with an occasional word from AFPC when I checked in weekly. Otis and Langley fell through so moving overseas seemed like a real possibility. We bought a few sweaters to deal with the northern European climate and Dutch language tapes.

Since I hadn't flown high-G aircraft for three years, I needed centrifuge training before climbing back into the F-15. There was a question about who would pay for this training; the losing unit or gaining unit. As the operations officer of the losing unit I knew funding centrifuge training would ruin our little detachment's budget. I pushed back hard insisting the gaining unit, 32 FS pay for it. I happened to see message traffic concerning this funding battle. In one message written by 32 FS, I read *"We are not sure Major Jones is coming to us"*. I called AFPC and asked them about the statement. Can you call back on a STU? (Secure telephone unit). Sure. When we were in secure mode, AFPC told me, it's not public knowledge, yet but Soesterburg is closing, so you won't be going there. How about Eglin? "I can do that." Sure; fly Eagles from the beaches of Florida's Emerald Coast? Throw me in that briar patch!

Chapter XI Eagles on the Beach

I soon received orders to attend Centrifuge training followed by the F-15 short (re-qual) course at Tyndall followed by assignment to the 59th Fighter Squadron, 33rd Fighter Wing, Eglin AFB, in Fort Walton Beach.

Re-qualifying in the F-15 at Tyndall gave me the opportunity to house-hunt on weekends. I found a nice home on a cul-de-sac in a small neighborhood just off Rocky Bayou in Niceville, FL. It had a nice big backyard with room enough for Laura's trampoline. We had the backyard fenced in for Kelly. We lived very close to a new bridge that spanned the huge Choctawhatchee Bay t across the middle dropping driving time to Destin and the Sugar-white beaches to thirty minutes.

We had great neighbors. The guys regularly played basketball in a neighbor's driveway that had been enlarged to make a decent half court with a high quality rim and backboard. Most games ended after the rest of the neighbors brought lawn chairs to watch and laugh at the rowdy games. One phone call to the local pizza delivery place created another block party.

As a joke, we purchased a gaudy plastic, pink flamingo with wire legs and decorated a neighbor's yard with it. Soon the flamingo made the rounds of the neighborhood winding up in peculiar places. Depending on the season or holiday the flamingo wore an appropriate costume.

The short course at Tyndall was still challenging because they were using C-models with the radar. The C-models also carried more internal fuel and faster computers. These C-model jets were a big step up from the A-models I flew with the 48th. But when I got to the 59th FS, I was in for a bigger treat. The 59th jets were not just C-models; they were MSIP (multi-stage improvement program) C-models. They were the last F-15Cs to come off the assembly line (the newest in the inventory). They were ten years newer than the A-models in the 48th. I personally had more flying time than these planes. They had the latest very high speed computers and all the latest avionics including the new APG-70 radar. Think about how newer technology changed your PC, your car, or your cell phone in ten years. That's the kind of leap the F-15 made between the A models of 1976 and the MSIP C-models of 1986. Their capabilities were staggering. They had more powerful engines, the new F-100-220s, with digital fuel controls which made them more reliable and less likely to hiccup with rapid throttle movement. The first big noticeable change was that these jets added the new AIM-120 AMRAAM (advanced medium range air-to-air missile to weapons load. This changed just about everything with respect to tactics. With the AIM-7, the launch aircraft had to remain locked to the target until impact to provide reflected radar energy on which the missile guided; once the AIM-120 gets close enough, it guides itself to impact. With the more advanced computers and radar, these newer jets tracked and designated multiple targets and launched multiple AIM-120s at them simultaneously. Once the missile gets close enough, the launch aircraft can drop its radar lock and leave. Its job is done. This launch and leave capability drove all new tactics for the F-15. I had much to learn.

My MQT at the 59th involved more than my requal course at Tyndall which wasn't teaching AMRAAM yet. I'd tell you all more about the jet but they'd lock me up and then hunt all of you down. These planes had so much amazing wizardry that we couldn't turn on all their stuff in our training areas over the Gulf of Mexico for fear that a Russian "fishing" trawler (the ones bristling with antennae) might learn something of their capabilities by sniffing the air for our strange emissions. We had simulators which let us play with all the toys.

I found the pilots in the 59th to have incredible skill at employing these killing machines. They took their jobs seriously and were determined to be the best in the world at it. In my assessment, they were. Over the years, the 59th has chalked up thirty seven aerial victories including several over Iraq. It was very cool to get off the crew van and step to a 59th jet with a green star painted on it, indicating an Iraqi MiG or Mirage kill. With my previous experience, I upgraded to flight lead quickly and was given the working call sign, Husky. After achieving MR status, the squadron graciously voted for me to keep "Spike" as my personal call sign. Then, inside the weapons Shop vault I stood on a short stool and signed "Spike Jones" on a piece of MiG wreckage suspended from the ceiling. I was now a full-up, 59th FS Lion. My official position was assistant operations officer.

In the early fall of my first year in the squadron; Lt Col Jim "Boomer" Boeme, the squadron commander told me that I was to be the project officer and deployed operations officer for the squadron's next rotation to Saudi Arabia for Operation Southern Watch (OSW) which was enforcement of the no-fly zone set up south of Bagdad after Desert Storm. This would be a great challenge and opportunity. But it was not to be. Several weeks before

Christmas, Boomer talked to me again. This time, to tell me the new Air Combat Command policy directing all field-grade (major and above) flying billets in the command had to be filled with officers who had met a RTF board. We had another major in the squadron, USAFA classmate, "Slugs" Smellie(his real last name) and Boomer didn't want to risk continuing to double-billeting us(a common practice) so he found a position for me as the Current Operations Flight Commander in the 33rd Operations Support Squadron(33 OSS). I was relieved that I wasn't going to be apart from my family during Christmas; but I was also disappointed at being left behind. I was anxious to get to the "Sandbox" and get in the game. On a subsequent rotation to OSW, the 59th FS was housed in a facility known as Kobar Towers (Sound familiar? Here's why -) when terrorist blew up an enormous truck bomb killing 22 Lions.

My new commander at the 33d OSS was Keith "Rubble" Risner. He resembled the Flintstones character. 33 OSS were the "Jokers." So that made Rubble the Chief Joker in the wing. That was about right. In the current operations flight we coordinated and scheduled the wing's shared assets like airspace, the paint barn, engine run facilities, and flying hours. We also maintained the ABDR (aircraft battle damage repair) bird. We had a gutted out F-F-15 that we beat up to simulate battle damage. Then maintainers patched the holes so we could beat it up again for more training. At some point the jet became too beat up to be useful so we coordinated with the State to have it carried out into the gulf and sank to make an artificial reef. The local fishermen loved this.

My main task was managing the 33d FW's flying

hour program. Wings are given O&M (operations and maintenance) funds based on the number of sorties and hours they fly in a fiscal year (1 Oct to 31 Sep). Before we started flying for the year; we were given X number of sorties and 1.3X hours (1.3 was our assigned average sortie duration or ASD). The F-15 costs $Z per hour to fly and maintain (and they ain't cheap). This equated to hundreds of millions per flying squadron. The 33d Fighter Wing had three.

With this kind of money in play, good stewardship demanded I track it daily.

So every morning I had computer print outs on my desk telling me how many sorties and hours the wing flew (pilots logged) the previous day. I tracked the burn rate to make sure we flew the right number of sorties and hours the previous day. I also monitored the actual ASD vs. the programmed ASD of 1.3 hours. It fouled things up if the pilots padded their personal flight logs by flying (logging) 2- hour missions of which the jets were capable.

If a squadron's ASD started to deviate too much from the plan, I'd calculated a new ASD to bring the squadron back in line. I'd call the squadron's operations officer and they made adjustments. ASD corrections could happen quickly by changing the aircraft's external tank configuration. We normally flew with a single, centerline external tank. When the ASD needed reduction, the fix was to remove this tank making the aircraft more maneuverable (=fun) and do a BFM surge. A BFM sortie burns fuel quickly because much of it is spent in full afterburner. (= more fun), resulting in sorties as short as .7 hours. Surging meant the squadron flew as many sorties as possible by refueling in the hot pits with engines running and going right back up for a second or third sortie without debriefing in between. Conversely, to increase the ASD, we could add external tanks, bring in a tanker and/or fly intercept only missions (pigs in space). For incentive, if a squadron met their flying hour program sorties and hours for the month, they earned the last Friday of the month off to make a three-day weekend.

If the wing made their flying hour program goals for the year, the last week in September was taken off. Of course, I had to account for these no-fly days in the annual program and for style points, I was expected to fly the last sortie of the program for the exact time remaining in the program on the last fly day of the year. This was Goldie Locks program execution – not too little, not too much; it had to be just right.

Whew! I deserved that week off. The side benefit to managing this program was I became very proficient at using Microsoft Excel. I also learned a lot about the business of operating a fighter wing at Eglin.

My hat's off to Colonels "Tunes" Looney and "Conan" Corley who did it and also stayed killing machines in the air.

Shirley's mother was fifty-five when we lost her to breast cancer. Shirley's older sister, Janet was diagnosed with breast cancer a year later at age, thirty-six. Shirley felt like she was just waiting for her turn so she decided to do something proactive about it. She elected to have a bilateral mastectomy. Angelina Jolie made headlines for a similar decision last year (2013). This was major surgery and my Mom drove over to help out around the house after Shirley left the hospital.

After several days, Shirley was still hurting and moving around slowly. She was also still feeling a touch queasy all the time. We called the surgeon's office and he wasn't concerned. He had given her some pretty potent anesthesia to keep her under for the seven-hour procedure. It was going to take some time for that stuff to get out of her system. One evening, Mom was cooking dinner which included Rice-a- Roni. Shirley got sick as soon as she smelled it. The run-down feeling and queasiness continued a few more days before Shirley sent me to the store for a home pregnancy test. She used it immediately and she tested positive.

How could this be? We're infertile! (Grace? Perhaps?) Uh-oh, what about the anesthesia? What would that stuff do to a baby? Before we panic; let's make sure she's really pregnant. I called a flight surgeon and made arrangements for Shirley to be seen the next day for a blood pregnancy test.

It was positive too. This was real. Shirley was pregnant! That last birth control pill she took fifteen years ago finally wore off.

We visited Shirley's surgeon about our concerns with the anesthesia. He calmed our nerves first by telling us the anesthesia used on Shirley was the same they would have used on a pregnant woman in a car accident. Then he pulled out his pregnancy due-date calculating wheel and determined while Shirley was in surgery, our baby was still enroute to the uterus, so since it hadn't snuggled in yet, it wasn't sharing Shirley's blood so it wasn't exposed to any narcotics during the surgery (even more grace!).

Doctor Archer explained, "We didn't do a routine pre-surgery pregnancy test because your records say you're infertile." Apparently not anymore!

Let's back up just a bit and let Shirley tell this miraculous part of our life together in a short story she wrote titled Mom's Eyes:

MOM'S EYES

For years my husband and I suffered the pain of infertility. Disappointing monthly cycles turned into years of waiting. After being told we had a one in a million chance of conceiving naturally, we looked toward adoption. Just nine short months later, our daughter's birthmother placed her in our arms. We felt so blessed and knew God had His hand in forming our family. Years later, I was suffering another kind of pain. I was losing my mother to cancer. My mother was the epitome of a matriarch, the nucleus of our family. One of my fondest memories of her is her eyes. She had the most beautiful blue eyes. They were so blue, they were nearly transparent. They were her most striking feature and made an impression on everyone she met. Throughout Mom's battle with cancer, my family prayed hard and often.

We asked for healing. We asked for more time. Then, as her suffering grew worse, we asked for less time. Mom slipped into a coma. Although unable to respond, we could tell she was aware of our presence. She remained in a coma for two days, unable to even open her eyes. A family member stayed with her around the clock.

As we realized we were spending our last morning

with her, we began our good-byes. I felt panicky knowing that in a few short minutes, I would have to begin living life without my mother.

I could hardly comprehend it. I would never again hear her voice on the other end of a telephone, I'd never hug her again and I would never see those eyes again. Under my breath, I began pleading with God. I knew she was dying and I was willing to let her go because her pain would finally end.

But I needed one thing. I needed to see her eyes. I felt I could face all that was ahead if I could just look into her eyes once more.

Please God, for all we've been through, I'm not asking much. Please, before she dies, let her open her eyes one last time. Mom's breathing changed and I knew we only had her a few more moments. She died peacefully, never opening her eyes.

Two and half years later, I was suffering yet again. After being married for fifteen years, I was in labor! I was about to give birth to our "one in a million"! Although the pain of infertility never leaves, I had learned to live with missing out on the privilege of pregnancy. We had given up. My husband and I were thrilled with our role as parents raising our 10 year old daughter. She was a blessing and filled us with joy. Life was all mapped out. We were content. When we learned I was pregnant, we were stunned. I never thought I would hear those words and it was difficult believing they were true. And now it was real, I was inside a delivery room. Labor was tough. And although there were moments when I thought it would never end, I refused pain medication, not wanting to miss a thing. I was graciously suffering the joy of childbirth.

Finally, the last push came and I was seconds from meeting my son. The nurse quickly handed him to me. He was squirming and screaming. My husband and I quickly ran through every parent's checklist counting fingers and toes. He was perfect. As he settled in my arms, I studied his face. Who would he look like? He snuggled in and began to relax.

We watched as he struggled to open his eyes against the light. When his eyes finally opened, mine filled with tears.

I begged God years before for one more glimpse of my mother's eyes. I thought he chose to ignore that simple request. I never imagined he would answer that prayer through a child I thought I would never have. The eyes I longed to see one more time for just one brief moment are the eyes I have looked into every day for the last nineteen years. I'm amazed at God's greatness, compassion, and grace.

Me again: Before we knew the baby's gender, we had a hard time coming up with girl names because Rick and Karen had taken all the good ones. (They had five daughters between them.) If it were a boy, Shirley wanted to name him Jacob because her maiden name was Jacobs. It sounded a bit Hebrew to me but I'm good with Jacob. His middle name would be mine. So if we had a boy, his name would be Jacob Michael Jones. Weeks later, it was time for a sonogram and we discovered unmistakable evidence that Jacob was in there. We had a still photo taken from the video. It was a bit grainy but if you looked at it long enough, you figured it out.

For Christmas that year we went to Orange Park to celebrate. Our parents lived a few blocks from each other in the Grove Park neighborhood Christmas morning; we opened gifts at my parent's house along with Rick, Karen, and their families. For my father's gift, Shirley and I put the sonogram of Jacob in a Christmas card, and wrote" it's a boy" on the inside. At first, he was puzzled to be handed a card rather than a gift-wrapped box like everyone else. He examined the envelope with curiosity and suspicion. When he opened the card, he stared at it a while trying to make sense of the photo. I watched from across the room as it slowly came into focus and what we wrote made sense with the photo. "It's a boy!" he shouted springing to his feet in front of his six granddaughters. It was the best gift we ever gave him.

As he left the room for another cup of coffee, He said, "I need to change my will."

It was assignment time again but this time around, the Air Force was trying something new, again. Available assignments were posted on the Internet and members could look for assignments they wanted and volunteer for them.

By now, I had been commissioned fifteen years and had yet to go overseas, so I was considered "hot" for an overseas short tour which usually meant Korea without your family. I called AFPC and asked, "If I find myself a long tour overseas, Will you turn it off to send me on a short tour?" No; if you find a job you like overseas, long, I we won't turn it off. There weren't a lot of appealing overseas jobs on the net.

I saw one for the 32d Air Operations Squadron at Ramstein AB, Germany but I really didn't understand what it did. Unbeknownst to me, 33FW commander, Col "Tunes" Looney had sent a letter of recommendation to Major General Cliver(also an F-15 pilot), the two-star Director of Operations for US Air Forces Europe(USAFE),pronounced, you safe EE. General Cliver passed the endorsement letter to the commander of the 32d Air Operations Group who passed it down to the commander of the 32d Air Operations Squadron, Lt Col John "Whistle" Entwhistle who asked the officers in the squadron if anyone knew a Major Spike Jones. Captain Jeff "Bodine" Ellis spoke up. I flew T-38s with Bodine at Randolph. He put in a good word for me and then gave me a call. Spike, you gotta get out here, this is great. We get MAJCOM (major command) staff credit but we wear bags (flight suits) every day. We don't go TDY (temporary duty) that often but when we do, it's to cool places.

A TDY is like a military business trip. The Navy calls it TAD. I talked to Shirley about moving to Germany and we figured we could hack it so I volunteered and soon had orders to the 32d Air Operations Squadron, Ramstein AB, Germany; but first I had to attend the Joint Air Operations Staff Course at Hurlburt Field on the other side of Ft. Walton Beach, where I DGed again.

Time passed and Shirley grew large. Then in April of '95 on a Sunday afternoon, Shirley went into labor. Jacob was born at midday, Wednesday. Shirley and I were exhausted.

Jacob didn't say how he felt but he slept a lot, so he must have been tired too. Even though Shirley's surgeon waylaid our fears about the anesthesia, we were still relieved when he came out with the requisite number of body parts attached where they were supposed to be; no missing parts, no extra parts, just a perfect blonde-haired, blue-eyed mini-me.

By this time, Kelly was fourteen years-old. She had gray on her muzzle and her eyesight was going, but she was still smart as a whip and a beloved member of the family and neighborhood. We were concerned about what to do with her if we were stationed overseas.

Laura gets in on the fun after my last
flight with the 59th FS June, 1995

We thought the trip and possible quarantine might be too much for her and it would be difficult to find a new home for such an old dog.

One morning before I left for work, Shirley called me to the garage where Kelly slept. Kelly was disoriented and had lost her balance. Shirley took her to the vet as soon as they opened but they couldn't determine what was wrong with her. During my break for lunch, we went back to the vet to check on her but nothing had changed. We decided to put her down rather than have her suffer like she was.

I was present when she took her first breath and I wanted to be there for her last, so I held her across my lap and told her what a good dog she was the vet administered the drugs to put her to sleep. I loved that sweet dog so much that I can't type these words nineteen years later without crying.

CHAPTER XIII
WOLFHOUNDS

We shipped a car overseas early so it would be there when we arrived. We were required to have passports for everyone. Jacob's was rejected because his little blue eyes were closed in the photo. (I told you he slept a lot!) So we hustled to get a new photo and I raced to New Orleans (the closest passport office) to walk his paperwork through.

With his new passport in hand, I rushed back to Eglin.

At eleven weeks- old, Jacob boarded a flight (with the rest of us) to Philadelphia for a connection to Frankfort, Germany. Travelling overseas with a ten year-old and an infant was a chore. Airline food choices don't include Enfamil, so we had to haul Jacob's formula and bottles with us. My sponsor, Major Don (Mobes) Mobley, met us at the airport and demonstrated the art of Autobahn driving on the very quick ride to Ramstein. I deposited my family at the TLF (temporary living facility) on base to rest while Mobes introduced me around the squadron.

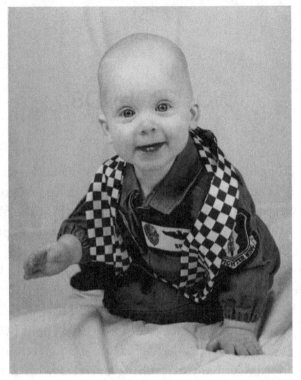

Jacob, 1996

I met my new boss; a big, blonde, Texan named Danny "DB" Burrows. How he squeezed into the tiny F-16 confounds me. He is a true Texan. He is also a believer. Here was another Christian fighter pilot. Now you've heard of two. There was also good friend, USAFA and Sunday school classmate, Major Kenny (Pogo) Dressel - F-16 pilot and fellow believer. [3]. Whip is a believer too. [4]. Tanker Pilot Mark (Molive) Olive is also a believer (but not a fighter pilot) although he could swap verbal jabs with the best of us. Then there was Sunday school classmate and F-15E front-seater, Dennis,

"Moose" Northcut. [5]. I forgot to mention Evan "Pins" Roelofs in the 59th. FS [6]; and Good Troll Buddy, Mike (Izod) Naye [7], who flew with me in the 48th FS. My new squadron was in the woods across the main drag from Headquarters, USAFE which was also Headquarters for NATO's AIRCENT.

32 AOS was once 32 FS, the greedy F-15 squadron at Soesterburg to which I was almost assigned. After 32 FS deactivated, it was re-activated as the 32 AOS. The 32 FS mascot was the Irish wolfhound so a Disney cartoonist's rendition of a big slobbering dog adorned the squadron patch.

Squadron heraldry follows a unit through its various incarnations through Air Force history. Awards and other memorabilia get passed along, through the years, as well.

As I walked through my new squadron, I was pleasantly surprised to find two Hughes Trophies atop a bookcase in a hall.

The Hughes trophy is presented by the Hughes corporation annually (they made the AIM-7 missile) to recognize an F-15 squadron for outstanding achievement. After our second Long Arrow victory in three years, we were hopeful to win the Hughes in the 48th FS. (*We should have!*) When I met my new squadron commander, "I said; "Sir, we need to get those Trophies out of the hall and display hem prominently in the squadron lobby. Or I could take them home." When I left the 32d in 1998, the trophies were in a display case in the squadron's lobby. I always said the three years spent in the 32d AOS were the most interesting of my career. I still hold to that claim.

What did the wolfhounds do? Simply put; the 32d AOS along with sister squadrons the 32d Air Intelligence squadron (32 AIS) and the 1st Combat Communications squadron (1 CCS) made up the 32d Air operation Group. (32 AOG). 32 AOG was tasked to provide a deployable Joint Air and Space Operations Center (JAOC) capability for USAFE and NATO. JAOCs plan, task, and direct Joint air operations in accordance with Joint Publication 3-56.1. (Our bible). Remember that ATO thing I talked about when I was an ALO at Ft Stewart? We put those together and monitored their execution using a warehouse full of computers with specialized software and communications equipment.

When it came to JAOCs and the processes, hardware, and software making them tick; we were the "Pros from Dover." and we received much attention. Since 32 AOG fell under the USAFE/DO, Maj Gen Cliver; we became the perfect pool of action officers to manage countless projects coming down from above.

32 AOS provided the core manning of a deployed JAOC with the other hundreds of required positions being filled by other officers throughout Europe. These folks need to be trained. I was tasked to develop the USAFE JFACC Training Course. Every Quarter we hosted hundreds of officers from all over Europe and gave them three days of training (Death by PowerPoint; we joked) we didn't have the equipment or facilities for hands-on training. That would come with the exercises we conducted either at our compound or the Warrior Prep Center (WPC) in nearby Einsiedlerhoff.

In the Nineties, many former Soviet bloc countries were interested in joining NATO. To make their transition easier, they sought to learn how the West provides command & control (C2). What better way to learn than to be taught by the Pros from Dover (Ramstein)? We sent small training teams to these countries and I was blessed to have made several of these trips.

My most memorable was to Romania. We flew into a former MiG base outside Bucharest and were treated like distinguished visitors. We drove through the Ploesti oil fields, the sight of horrific 9th Air Force bomber losses during WWII raids to cut off Hitler's supply of petroleum.

It felt like hallowed ground to me as we drove though, knowing hundreds of fellow airmen lost their lives in and above these fields. We were on our way to the Romanian Air Force Academy in the Carpathian Mountains. We stopped briefly at one of Vlad the Impaler's (Dracula's) castles on the way.

On another trip we visited the Hungarian Air Defense headquarters. This time we flew into Budapest and drove to Veszprem near Lake Balaton (one of the largest lakes in Europe.) In Veszprem we were treated very well. I had recently been promoted to Lt Col., the senior member of our training team. My room at the hotel was large with a huge rooftop terrace overlooking the city. Our interpreter (most likely an intelligence agent) escorted us everywhere. He took us up to a citadel near the hotel that sat on top of a hill. The walled citadel compound included an ancient cathedral.

After touring the church we looked over the wall at the city below. Recognizing that we weren't locals, an old woman in a worn coat and a scarf pulled tightly over her gray head asked our interpreter about us. He explained that we were Americans. She smiled and her clear gray eyes sparkled as she said, "Ah, America!" She then looked down, shook her head in disgust, and said," Ah, Clinton" This was shortly after the Monica Lewinski story had broken. In less than 60 seconds, my American pride soared, then crashed.

One An "Air Force appreciation" trip included several wolfhounds; Moose, Molive, and Major Mike "Rolly" Rollison a B-1 offensive weapons officer.

Rolly, Spike, Molive, Moose, & Wayno aboard
the USS Nassau, The flags say, 32 AOS

We flew to Marseilles, France to meet the USS Nassau, an Amphibious Assault ship with Marines onboard. The Nassau looked like a miniature aircraft carrier but what was really fascinating about this type of ship was its ability to open and partially submerge the stern, permitting landing craft with Marine combat equipment or Navy SEALs with their rubber boats to launch and recover. The Marines had tanks, artillery, HMMWVs, attack helos, and AV-8 Harriers. (Just about everything you need for a small war.) The ship's flight deck was smaller and didn't have catapults since the helos and AV-8s took –off and landed vertically. During night ops, the ship was completely dark and the pilots of these bizarre aircraft used night vision goggles to see.

It was scary enough to watch (mostly listen to night flight ops from the bridge. To be doing it in an aircraft was just plane (get it?) insane. Thank God we have brave and skillful men willing to take that task on.

After a few days roughing it at the pier in Marseilles, we left to work an exercise off the coast of Sardinia using the JFACC Afloat concept, with the skipper of the Nassau acting as the JFACC. Lesson learned – *Never sit in the skipper's chair on the bridge.* Right, Molive? Rolly was the chief of Combat Plans and I was the Chief of Combat Operations, the two major divisions in a JAOC. Rolly and his folks produced and published the ATO. Once published, Combat Operations owned it for execution. The JFACC received two briefings a day related to the exercise in which we were engaged; One from Plans and one from Ops. With each briefing, Rolly and I took pot shots at each other. They became more and more complex and we spent way too much time playing with PowerPoint's features trying to outdo each other. Fortunately, the skipper, amused by our antics, let us continue.

Anyone remember the Chinese embassy that was accidentally bombed in Sarajevo? Guess who planned that one, Pogo. 32 AOS deployed to Vicenza, Italy for two months to plan, task, and direct joint air operations over Bosnia- Herzegovina in 1996.

After we were settled in to our home in Landstuhl,

Germany, Shirley had a post-partum checkup and the physician found the same endometriosis preventing her from pregnancy was still present. The amazed doctor couldn't believe Shirley had conceived. With God's miraculous help; she did, and that little baby boy is now nineteen years-old, over six feet tall, and working on his BS in Network Security.

Jacob in our backyard in Carrollton

Jacob on Prom night 2013

My birthday that year (1996) fell on a Saturday and DB gave me the day off to walk over to Vicenza high school's football field and watch the Naples Wildcats beat the tar out of them. What a great birthday gift. I wonder who could have arranged all of that. While onboard the Nassau, Lt. Col. John "Motown" Larned, our new wolfhound commander, informed me I had been tagged to deploy to Saudi Arabia for three months in the spring. Great! I guess my turn was going to come up eventually.

I packed my deployment bag, including a new Discman for listening to CDs and flew into PSAB (prince Sultan Air Base), Al kharj, Saudi Arabia. PSAB was one of our primary bases for OSW. The rotator on which I flew landed after dark and the folks we replaced boarded as soon as we were clear of the aircraft. The only Saudi citizen I saw was the customs guy. I wore my flight suit, lugging my deployment bag when I approached him. You pilot? He asked. "Yes sir," I responded. OK; he waved me through. I was disappointed I didn't experience any Saudi culture. I did experience Saudi weather; hot during the day, cold at night, dry, and windy. I also ran into some Saudi wildlife – a lizard called a dub. It stayed hydrated in the desert by absorbing what little moisture there was out of the air. I worked as the chief of the combat operations center set up in a trailer near the base's command post. I maintained contact with the JAOC in Riyadh and broke out the ATO for the squadrons to build their flying schedules. My first task was to use the few officers who worked with me to write checklists for our replacements. We had no checklists. Once we completed this, it became apparent we had more people than we really needed so I devised a work schedule allowing more time in the gym or working other projects. I lived in Tent City; several acres of desert covered with canvas GP (general purpose) medium tents. Each tent held cots for eight. Down the center of the tents were wooden pallets covered in old worn-out Asian carpets. At the front of the tent was either a dusty old sofa or a couple of dusty upholstered chairs or both for those assigned to the tent to watch TV. The showers and latrines were a few hundred yards away just outside the asphalt road which encircled Tent City. We had a chapel (but no cross could be displayed), a gym, a chow tent, and a small base exchange. We also had bunkers (We were within scud range of Iraq) I was the commander of bunker number eleven.

At PSAB I was able to call the Ramstein operator a get a phone patch to our home in nearby Landstuhl. I also had e-mail which is how Motown let me know that I was the new 32d AOS operations officer. My goal at PSAB was to get back in shape. I lifted weights daily, ran daily until the pain in my hips forced me to walk and then ride a recumbent bicycle. I sunbathed between the tents while listening to Point of Grace CDs. I lost twenty five pounds, bulked up, and sported a pretty good tan, when I returned home. My hips were really bothering me to the point that I sought medical attention back at Ramstein. I explained how I had been injured playing basketball in Vicenza months before. I managed to do the splits all the way down to the court that any Olympic gymnast would have been proud of. The flight doc thought it was might be a severe groin pull that needed more time to fully heal.

When I returned from Saudi, someone offered to keep the kids for a few days so Shirley and I drove down the hill from our home to the train station in Landstuhl. We took the train to Paris and then travelled one stop on the subway. We emerged on the Champs E`lysees; a short walk from the French Officer's Club where we spent four days – just the two of us. Besides the Louvre and Notre Dame, my favorite part of Paris was the hot crepes cooked and sold right on the streets. Living only four hours away by car; we visited Paris many times. That was one of the great things about being stationed at Ramstein. With its central location and the autobahn system; you could be in half a dozen countries in as many hours. For us in Landstuhl, France was thirty only 30 minutes away. Belgium, Luxemburg, and the Netherlands were close enough for a weekend trip.

One spring we drove to Berlin for a few days and then south through Dresden and on to Prague where we stayed in an apartment across the street from and maintained by the US embassy. All the sights were a short walk away.

Shirley became comfortable enough to go solo on bus tours. When she wanted Polish Pottery, she borrowed Jacob's wagon and took a base tour bus to Poland.

I spent a week TDY in Poland for a US-Polish exercises where I taught US C2 procedures to polish officials while our F-15s trained against Polish MiGs.

While TDY back at Vicenza, Italy toward the end of my tour with the 32d; I learned that I had been selected by a USAFE Squadron Commanders board. This was a big deal and I had no idea this board was meeting. Brig Gen Hal Hornburg, future 4-star commander of Air Combat Command personally delivered the news to me. He was stationed at Vicenza at the time. Unfortunately, no F-15 squadrons in Europe needed commanders at the time.

Maj Gen Mike Short, SAFE/DO after Gen Cliver, worked behind the scenes on my behalf to get a flying job for me when my time in USAFE ended. When I was promoted to Lt Col; he told me his job was to get me off the staff and back into the flying business to make a run for squadron command. Sounds good to me, boss. So I was assigned to the 25th FTS at Vance AFB, OK where

I flew T-38s for pilot training and my first assignment eons ago.

Getting back to the States was difficult. I was involved with a huge biennial exercise at the WPC working twelve-hour shifts. One afternoon, I received a message to phone home. When I did, Shirley told me her sister, Janet was hospitalized and experiencing the "beginning of the end." She had been battling breast cancer for a long while. I made arrangements for Shirley and Jacob to fly out immediately. Laura and I would catch up after the exercise concluded. Thank God, she was old enough to look after herself while I worked.

Janet died before Laura and I left Germany but at least Shirley made it home in time for her funeral. Janet (thirty days my senior) was only forty years-old when she died, leaving a nine year-old daughter, Katie, behind.

"Oklahoma!" Laura moaned, "I don't want to live in Enid, Oklahoma!" "You'll love it," I said. "I'll bet you have a pair of cowgirl boots within two years." No way!

I won that bet. Before moving to Enid we had to spend some time in San Antonio. For me to go through T-38 PIT yet again. We found a small two bedroom apartment near Randolph and settled in for a brief stay We entered Laura into a summer program at Sea World to help pass the time faster for our thirteen year-old. Soon; with current IP certification in my flight records and a few more T-38 hours under my belt, we said goodbye to Randolph, San Antonio, Lori Schmitt, and the penguins at Sea World to head North on I-35.

Enid hadn't changed much since we left twelve years earlier, and Vance AFB was practically identical. We moved into the TLF while we looked for a house to call home. We found a keeper on Quail Ridge on the other side of the wheat field in which Kelly ran. Knowing there were lakes in the area, I considered buying another sailboat. My mistake was mentioning this idea to Shirley, who, knowing how hot it could get in Oklahoma, considered a backyard swimming pool, instead; being sly, she said we'd put it to a family vote. Laura (*13*) and Jacob (*3*) had never been on a sailboat but they had been in pools so I was easily outvoted three to one and I soon learned how to get the water Ph spot- on and maintain crystal clear water in our new kidney –shaped pool.

Take a look at those ages again. Shirley lived in a foreign country with her husband off TDY to other foreign countries much of the time with children of those ages. She handled *puberty* and *potty training* at the same time! *Alone!*

Looking back, the pool was the right way to go. It cost about half what a sailboat would have cost and we used it a lot more than we would have used a boat.

One summer we hired a college student to teach swimming lessons. All the moms in the neighborhood came over and drank coffee in our breakfast nook and watched their little ones learn to swim. After a day of flying in 100 degree heat, I used to go into my bedroom, get out of my nasty sweat stained flight suit and quietly slip into the pool to cool off. If Jacob caught me, he'd soon be in there with me and I'd get my workout throwing him up in the air.

This time around; Enid broke a record set back in 1980 for consecutive days over 100 degrees F.

CHAPTER XIV
BACK TO PILOT TRAINING

The 25th FTS Commander, Lt Col "Torch" Urban, a believer and former F-111 pilot [8] (You're still counting aren't you?); came to meet us at the house after we moved out of the TLF. One of the first things he asked us was, "Have you found a church home yet?" Then he invited us to attend his church, Immanuel Baptist. Shirley and I attended Immanuel when we first moved to Enid for pilot training.

At the 25th, I was assigned to H Flight commanded by Major "Pins" Roelofs (You already counted him in the 59th FS.) I did the same job as a Lt Col that I did as a 2Lt; which was great! I was an *old guy* compared my students and flew my butt off! Tony Villalobos [9] was another IP in the squadron. Tony and wife, Audrey lived in our neighborhood, attended Immanuel, and were active in OCF at USAFA.

Jacob started preschool at Immanuel's Christian school (Audrey was his teacher.) Laura enrolled at Oklahoma Bible Academy (OBA) just down the road from our house. Immanuel was a great church. Senior Pastor, Wade Burleson, emphasized the message of grace:

There is nothing we can do to earn our way into God's favor including spending eternity with Him in heaven (the ultimate expression of His favor). Jesus Christ did all the work for us by taking our place and obediently dying on the cross.

Our Sunday school class teacher, Dan Wolever, owned and operated a hair styling shop. He was a hoot and a thorough bible teacher. He knew his stuff. What I loved best about the class was its diversity. We had an Air Force Pilot, a Chiropractor, a hair dresser, a cardio-pulmonary surgeon. And Wally, an old guy who shot sporting clays with a 410 as well as the rest of us did with 12-guage shotguns. I also loved that Dan wasn't afraid of the tough stuff –doctrine. The guys in the class introduced me to hunting.

It started with an invitation to go to a sporting clay range. I agreed but explained I didn't have a shotgun. No problem, they said, we'll find one for you. They loaned me a shot gun but it was old-school with not so much as a rubber pad on the stock's butt. We used 12 gauge shot guns and my loaner kicked like a mule. We shot on the 100 clay course and the 50 clay course. My shoulder was black and blue.

Then one September afternoon, I received a call at work. Hey, today is opening day of dove season and we're going hunting. Want to go? "Sure but I'll need to borrow a shot gun again but not that elephant gun I used before." We've got you covered. Can you meet us at five? "I'll be there." I was, and we drove out east of town to some land the surgeon owned that had its crop plowed under to attract the birds. They gave me a stool, a box of shells, and planted me by a fence post. You know what dove look like, don't you? "Doesn't everyone?" "I just don't eat them." Then Brian the surgeon said, "Here, try this," as he handed me his Benelli Super Black Eagle semiautomatic twelve- gauge. It's the Maserati of shot guns; Italian, very expensive, very light weight, and next to no recoil. I bagged a few dove and became a huge Benelli fan.

The guys took me pheasant and duck hunting as well and I was soon hooked. I loved getting up early to be set up in the blinds before sun-up. Watching the earth come alive for the day in the cold morning air was awesome.

My most memorable student this time around was Sarah Tobin. Not because she was female. I had several female students before her.

In my experience, the only difference between male and female student pilots was the pitch of their voices over the intercom. Sarah, saw my being assigned as her primary IP as a sign. She wanted to fly the F-15. She was a very experienced civilian pilot, - a CFII. (Certified Flight Instructor Instructor); the civilian equivalent of what I was at PIT. She taught people how to teach people to fly. This was impressive but civilian flying doesn't translate to military flying. Sarah had trouble getting through what I called the 300 knot barrier. She was fine handling the slow speeds of civilian aircraft and performed well enough in Primary training in the Navy's T-34 (She went through primary in a Navy slight training squadron at NAS Whiting Field near Pensacola.)to be selected for the T-38 track. But the T-38 rarely flew less than 300 knots and as high as 500 knots to begin some aerobatics.

Sarah had the annoying habit of underlining her mistakes by saying, "Oopsie!" This did not display the professionalism or confidence required of an Air Force pilot. Sarah holds the dubious distinction of being the only student I ever had to wash out of pilot training.

She was, however, recommended for further technical training; so she went to Tyndall AFB to train as an air weapons controller. I hope she found her niche and is enjoying a long and successful Air Force career.

Flying T-38s two and three times a day as an old guy couldn't last long. Eventually, someone would find out how much fun I was having and put a stop to it.

I had accumulated over3, 000 hours in the T-38 when I was appointed the 71ˢᵗ FTW Chief of Plans. This put me in charge of a small team who maintained the wing's plans and, conducted exercises to evaluate the wing's ability to execute them.

These were plans for dealing with disasters such as aircraft accidents, train derailments, terrorist attacks, Y2K internet and computer catastrophes, etc. These plans were the basis for checklists we developed for use by the battle staff of which I was the director.

One afternoon, Colonel Gary Ballentine, the vice wing commander stopped me in the hall outside the command post and told me they wanted me to take command of o the 8ᵗʰ FTS, one of the T-37 squadrons. It was a Tweet squadron, but *it was a flying squadron command!* Praise God! I get to go through PIT again! – That makes twice in a year! (They should give medals for that.) Praise God again!

This fourth time through PIT was my easiest yet. Being a Lt. Col. and current IP helped. Being a squadron Commander-select helped even more. I got the unofficial Executive course.

USAFA Classmate, Lt. Col. Bill Franklin was being transferred from C-130Hercules Pilot duties to the 8th; so not only were we USAFA and PIT classmates, we were future squadron mates. Bill was a straight shooter with a wife and eight children waiting for him up in Enid. We helped each other through the course and became good friends. The 8th FTS was part of the new Joint Specialized Pilot Training Program. (JSUPT).

In this program the students were USAF, USN, and USMC officers as were the IPs. Command of the squadron alternated between USAF (fighter pilot preferred) and USN officers (carrier pilot preferred) every year. Prior to taking command an officer served as operations officer for a year, then moved up to the command billet for a year. The other T-37 squadron was the 33rd FTS. Both Tweet squadrons shared one building and the one hundred plus T-37s on the noisy flight line. We also shared the airspace, the runways, the traffic pattern, and the parking lot. I played operations officer to USN Commander; "Splash" Coy, a Tomcat pilot I probably gunned repeatedly when he flew out of Oceana. The operations officer in the 33rd was USN Commander Mike Shea (Touché), a Prowler pilot (I never tangled with Prowlers and probably would have passed if I'd been given the opportunity. (It would be like clubbing baby seals.).)Touché was a good quail and pheasant hunting partner. We had offices beside each other, next to the operations desk where we could keep an ear out for what was going on.

We had fun exchanging verbal jabs and pranks all day. *Never, ever* leave a coffee cup unattended when Touché is around.

The next USN officer selected to replace me as commander of the 8th was Commander Dave "Swat" Swathwood, an S-2 Viking pilot. Swat was always quick with a joke or funny comment. He was hilarious. Except for this one time:

When Swat finished PIT; he came back up to Enid and visited the squadron. Right before he came into my office, I heard Splash talking in hushed tones to the Supervisor of Flying at the operations desk. The conversation didn't sound good.

I poked my head out of my office and made eye contact with Splash. "Is something up?" He came into my office and closed the door. Yeah, there's a smoking hole out there right now. "Do we know who it is?" "Is it one of ours?" Yeah, it's a solo student out of A Flight, Ensign Crohn. The ensign badly overshot the landing runway (He was only half way through his final turn when he crossed the extended centerline of the runway.) and attempted to make an instantaneous 90 degree turn to line up with the runway. The aircraft couldn't turn that tightly at such a slow speed with gear, flaps, and speed brake hanging. It stalled and spun into the ground about a mile from the runway. Ensign Crohn was killed on impact. His passing and memorial service was tough on the squadron, especially his fellow students in A Flight. Shirley was picking Jacob up from preschool and saw the rising smoke on the airfield.

Unaware of what had just happened; Swat chose this exact time to come into my office, introduce himself, and say, "So – how do you like the job so far?"

In Enid, this time; I tried running again, but my

hips were just too painful. I finally wised-up and went to see the flight surgeon, fearful that any medication he might suggest would ground me. Instead, he referred me to an orthopedist at Tinker AFB, in Oklahoma City. The specialist took several X-Rays and displayed them on the light board to show me my problem. There was a noticeable gap between the ball at the top of my femur and my hip bone socket on both sides. You have osteoarthritis in both hips. See those? Those are bone spurs. I bet that hurts! "So how do we fix it?" Hip Replacement but you're too young. "So, what do I do?" Drugs. "Can I fly with those?" Sure, no problem. He prescribed 200 mg/day Bextra (read: horse pill) which replaced Celebrex after it was pulled from the market. The Bextra helped some, but I was still hurting. Climbing in and out of the jet was painful.

CHAPTER XV
IT'S GOOD TO BE KING

One of the best perks for being in command of a flying squadron on a small base with only four flying squadrons is the parking. There's reserved parking everywhere, but the most important parking space was in front of the squadron. As soon as I was able, I wondered into C Flight. There it was - the Block Award; looking every bit as ugly as it did 18 years earlier.

I was pleased to discover Splash had started our First Friday celebrations. On the first Friday of every month; we stopped flying a little early, ordered dozens of pizzas and relaxed in the squadron lounge. We used this time for "Hails and farewells." My only change was to include the students and all family members. I wanted the students to feel like they had a stake in the 8th. If it felt like their squadron too, they would perform better. This also went for their spouses.

Spike &Splash outside the 8th FTS

Shirley met with the student wives regularly and they benefitted from her experience. Following Shirley's lead, many student wives joined the officers' spouse club setting membership records for Vance.

Crud is a noncontact (for the most part) sport common to USAF fighter organizations world-wide. In nearly every O' Club in the Air Force you'll find a billiard table for playing crud.

Only two balls are required; the cue ball and a striped object ball. Two teams play against each other trying to illuminate players on the opposite team. This is done by shooting the cue ball by hand at the object ball while a member of the opposing team defends by distracting the shooter after having done all he could to keep the shooter from retrieving the cue ball and getting to the shooting end of the table for a valid shot. If the shooter knocks the object ball in a pocket, the defense was clearly inadequate and the defender loses a life. If the object ball stops after having travelled at least six inches before the next shooter in sequence can retrieve the cue ball and shoot from the proper end of the table, the new shooter losses a life After losing three lives, you're out of the game. The game continues in this manner until attrition takes the teams down to one versus one. The last man standing determines which team wins. Lives can be lost for grabbing the corner of the table to help propel oneself around the corner; not shooting from the end of the table; the flight suit zipper must be inside the 45 degree lines made by the folded felt on the corners of the shooting end of the table. Accidentally bumping into the referee costs a life; as will any act the referee decides warrants punitive damages such as shooting or defending out of order, touching any ball on the table other than the cue ball, or causing someone to spill their beverage. During my time as skipper (as the USN and USMC officers called me) of the 8th FTS, we won the 71st FTW Crud tournament. Yeehaw!

In the O'Club at our first Christmas party, some of the 8th ladies, including Shirley decided they wanted to play cud. I refereed. Wearing their formal attire; they played every bit as rough as the guys and enjoyed the game enough that they wanted to meet at the Club once a week to play. I joined them to teach the game and referee.

Pretty soon, the 8the arranged to have a 71st FTW

Ladies Crud Tournament. We found another billiard
table and had it installed in the Club which was packed
that night setting an all-time club attendance record. It
was clear from the start that our ladies were the team
to beat. They fell short of winning, coming in second
place; but I couldn't have been prouder of Shirley and her
eightballer ladies sporting their custom LadyEightballers
Crud team T-shirts. All wasn't wine and Roses in the 8th;
not with Touché in the building. One day I walked into
my office after flying and found what looked like Cocoa
Puffs all over my desk. The 33rd (Touche's squadron) had
a fund raiser where they bought votes; with the winner
receiving a young goat. I wound up with a goat and
Touche's squadron made money off of it! touché`, Touché.

Fortunately, I drove my small pickup to work that
day. I loaded the goat in the back and went home. Mike
and Kim "Burly" Shea lived down the street from us on
Quail Ridge. They had cute little girls who would love
a baby goat (Who wouldn't, besides me?) I took the goat
for a walk that evening after dinner and quietly tied it to
the girls' swing set in the Shea backyard. The next day I
drove by and the goat was still there.

One of the really cool things Splash set up when he
skippered was a program where we sent two T-37s with
four IPs to NAS Jacksonville to meet with a group of
T-45s (USN's advanced trainer) students and IPs. The
students were there for carrier qualification, for which
they had been training for weeks. The IPs led three
students (who were solo) to a carrier out in the Atlantic.
After three successful traps, they were qualified and sent
back to Jax. Our IPs sat in the back seat of the T-45 and

we rode along as observers. The Enterprise (CV-65 not NC-1701) was the carrier when my turn for a boondoggle home came. I was a little surprised at the lack of training I received on the T-45. I guess they reasoned that I'd figure out how to strap in correctly and pull an ejection handle if the situation for its use presented itself. The first thing I noticed that was different about this particular jet was its ride on the taxiway. I felt every expansion crack in the pavement. I mentioned this to my chauffer. He told me the tires were over pressurized for carrier ops. At the ship we flew what I expected by way of an overhead pattern. I saw "the "ball" (a lighting system used to help pilots judge their approach.) The touchdown was firm and the stop was sudden as expected. We crossed to the other side of the flight deck to refuel with our engine running. Then we waited our turn for the catapult. The whole time we sat there; the IP told me he was logging flight time since the engine was running. Our time came and we hooked up to the shuttle. I knew enough to press my head back hard and keep my hands clear of the controls. This was a good thing because I hadn't been briefed on anything. When the catapult did its thing, the acceleration was unlike anything I had ever experienced. My peripheral vision was a blur and my head shook violently. Violent is the best way I can describe launching from a carrier. It was very quick. The ride went from violent to smooth in an instant. Still not my cup of tea but thank God for men like "Stormin (Major Seip did an exchange tour in the F-14 before *upgrading* to the F-15 and the 48th) Splash, Touché and Swat who thrived on it.

Being piped aboard for my change of command

Time for our change of command ceremony came quickly, Splash and I wanted to do it with style so we found a military band at Fort Sill, OK willing to travel to Enid and play for us. We blended USAF and USN customs for a hybrid ceremony with live music; a first for Vance. Rick, my parents, and the Elliots (Jim and Anita, remember them?) flew out for the ceremony. When in command, an officer wears a command pin on his uniform. The USAF and USN command pins are different (gold vs. silver like our wings). But this was a joint squadron; Rick recognized this distinction by presenting me a Navy command pin engraved with my name and USAF. I couldn't legally wear it on my uniform but it is proudly displayed in my retirement shadowbox.

My objectives for command were simple. I would lead by example; being the best pilot and instructor in the squadron. I would represent the fighter and Christian communities in a positive manner. I would also find a way to make members of the 8th proud to be so. T-37 IPs were often looked down upon because of the jet they flew. I did some research on squadron heritage and discovered the 8th photo squadron flew F-5s (P-38 Lightnings modified with cameras instead of guns) during WWII in the south Pacific. I had our patch redesigned to better resemble the original. The original patch depicted a tomahawk-welding Native American standing behind an eight ball. Over the years, the Native American's face went from a fierce warrior look to an impish grin. The Air Force Heritage Office which had to approve the patch change, initially expressed concern that changing the patch would offend Native Americans. I countered with, *not* changing the patch would be offensive to native Americans. We ordered the new patch in bulk before it was officially approved. I had already decided we would wear them if they had been disapproved. Next we found some original members of the squadron and hosted a sixtieth anniversary bash at the club. I knew I was on to something with respect to squadron morale when I returned from a cross-country weekend to find my parking place at the squadron painted red(our squadron color) with our logo (eight ball with feathers) painted on it. Nice!

I flew as much as my meeting schedule allowed making sure I trip-turned (flew three times in a day) as well. If the line IP was working this hard, so would I. I also attended morning briefings; even those that started at oh, dark thirty. Donetta Hakman, my exceptional secretary was awesome about keeping me on time to my meetings while keeping me on the flying schedule.

Hunting is a way of life in Enid, OK. While there this time, I got hooked. Shirley surprised me one Christmas with my own Benelli, 12-guage shotgun so I could join the Sunday school guys on duck and geese hunts without having to ask for a loaner. Touché knew someone west of town who owned a lot of land. He and I joined up quite a bit to hunt quail and pheasant.

CHAPTER XVI

COLONEL WHO?

- ✓ MAJCOM Staff
- ✓ Joint experience
- ✓ Graduate degree
- ✓ USAFE squadron commanders list
- ✓ Flying Squadron Command
- ✓ Air War College
- ✓ Major flying competition win
- ✓ Multiple Top Gun Awards
- ✓ IP of the Year
- ✓ Multiple DG awards

It looks like I've got all the squares filled for one last promotion – to Colonel. But God had another way ahead. The promotion board has your whole record to review when rank ordering everyone in the zone for promotion. Due to the sheer number of records involved (thousands); an all-important form, the promotion recommendation form (PRF) is written to sum up an officer's career in bullet statements on one page. The PRF has three boxes to check: definitely promote (DP), promote (P), and do not promote (DNP).

Clearly, the box checked is a *huge* deal. Who decides which box to check? It depends on numbers. If there are enough Lt Cols in a wing to generate a large enough pool for comparison, the wing commander decides which box to check. If not, the candidates are pooled at the next higher level: the Numbered Air Force. Being a small base, Vance didn't have enough of Lt Cols to give Col Doug Raaberg, 71st FTW commander the responsibility to decide who gets the DPs; so my PRF along with those of candidates from most of the other pilot training wings were sent to HQ, 19th Air Force for its two-star commander to decide. When I received a copy of my PRF back with a "P" recommendation rather than a DP, I was crushed. I didn't think making Colonel was a forgone conclusion but I thought I had a very competitive record and no one would be surprised if I made it. I think most assumed I would make it.

Well, I didn't. Ouch! *God is in control. God has a plan.* My boss, 71st Operations Group Commander, Colonel "Waldo" Givhan; USAFA grad, F-15 pilot, and Alabama native (can't beat that!) said, "Air Force's loss." I appreciated that. I also appreciated that he left me in my command position. Not only that, but after I passed command to Swat. Colonel Givhan made me his deputy commander of the Operations Group. Shirley and I decided to hold our heads high and present ourselves as a class act in dealing with this enormous disappointment. We attended Laser Lazarski's promotion party (he made it) and I began looking for a job elsewhere.

Shirley & me, Christmas 2000

CHAPTER XVII

BACK TO FLORIDA

We kept up with the Rollisons (Rolly and Barb) after we left Germany. He was in this strange sounding organization at Hurlburt Field in Fort Walton Beach, FL called the Air Force Command and Control Training and Innovation Group or AFC2TIG. This unit was in the JAOC training business which was my other area of expertise (other than flying, foosball, crud, and Frisbottle.) I talked to Rolly, thinking it might be a good fit. He agreed. There were several Wolfhounds working there. Col Raaberg and Col Givhan pulled some strings and soon I had orders to Hurlburt to be the deputy commander, AFC2TIG.

Timing could have been better. Laura had literally just completed her SATs when we picked her up from the testing site and drove away from Enid between her junior and senior years at OBA. I had been able to fly cross country to house-hunt and found a nice house in a gated community near Hurlburt. It was still under construction so we were able to make some custom touches here and there. It's a long drive from northwest Oklahoma to the Florida panhandle. Florida's Emerald Coast has the most beautiful beaches in the world. It felt good to be back. When Jacob first saw the sand, he asked if it was snow.

We rented a condo on the beach while waiting for our house to be completed.

Laura left OBA (250 students total grades 8 through 12) to attend Niceville High School with two thousand in the student body.

Laura wore boots in Enid, 1999

Jacob attended Rocky Bayou Christian School. The large, dolphin-filled Choctawhatchee Bay with all its bayous demanded a Sailboat. There would be no pool/ boat vote this time. The community pool sat in the middle of the circular road on which our home sat. It was practically Florida Law to own a boat with water this beautiful. I knew exactly what I wanted and did quite a bit of Internet research to find the perfect boat for us.

I looked for something large enough for Jacob and I to sleep in but still small enough that it didn't break the bank. I wanted a trailerable boat so I could store it out of the water; negating the need for bottom paint and the hassle and expense of cleaning the nasty stuff that grows on boats in saltwater. Stability was important for Shirley's sake. She only just barely tolerated sailboats for my sake. Sailboats lean (heal) and Shirley didn't like it any better than Mom did. Speed is always important, so I wanted our boat to be quick. I found what I was looking for in the Precision 21. I discovered it online and crawled all over one at a dealer near Jacksonville. It was just what I was looking for.

On the way to the 2004 Mug Race finish line

She had bunks below for four, a portable marine head, sink w/ pump faucet, a small alcohol stove, a built in cooler, plenty of storage, and a 12 volt system for accessories like a marine stereo, fans, and lights. On the exterior she had high quality spars and running rigging. She seemed a bit over-engineered.

After I got her home, I pulled out her interior teak trim and applied several coats of a satin varnish. I used a high-gloss varnish on the teak handrails and beautiful teak and ash tiller. She had a bow rail, stern rail w/ built in seats and an integrated swim ladder plus lifelines all around. (all uncommon on a boat this small). Blue water Bay Yachts in Niceville is a Precision dealer so I drove over one day and ordered my very own Precision 21 with a 155% genoa (a large headsail) on a roller furler and a custom Precision mainsail cover.

We named the boat Tschuss! This is the informal German word for goodbye; like bye or see you, in English.

Post'l Point - a favorite spot to spend the night

Our German cleaning lady taught Jacob to say this because Aufwiedersehen was too big a mouthful for our toddler. To Shirley's dismay; I spared no expense when I outfitted the boat. West Marine loved me.

The AFC2TIG was as busy as its name was long. It was responsible for training numbered Air Force (NAF) commanders and their staff members in JAOC procedures and processes. Our primary tool for this training was Exercise Blue Flag. We had computers that could model and simulate ground forces (good and bad guys) and the air forces the NAF staff planned and tasked to use against the bad guys. We had subject matter experts "fly" the simulated sorties for realism. We had defense contractors (mostly retired military) provide over-the-shoulder training for the NAF staff members.

We also administered the AF Senior Mentor Program where retired general officers with JFACC experience worked with the NAF commanders. Maj Gen Short from USAFE was a Senior Mentor.

The AFC2TIG fell under the Air warfare Center (AWC) at Nellis AFB, NV. The AWC also runs the Air Force Weapons School as well as the Fighter Weapons School or more correctly the Fighter Weapons Instructor Course (FWIC). Not fighter-centric; the Air Force Weapons School trains the best of all our weapons systems operators. Rolly Rollison and his wife Barb are close friends despite his being a B-1 Weapons Systems Officer. Rolly is an Air Force Weapons School graduate which makes his ego as big as mine. We do not call FWIC Top Gun. We call it FWIC (pronounced, fwic) or just Weapons school. And I'm pretty sure they don't play volleyball there. The Rollisons were Wolfhound squadron mates in Germany and he helped me get my last assignment at Hurlburt Field where they were also assigned. Shirley and I had dinner with the Rollisons last night. This book came up in our discussion and we decided a certain incident needed to be told:

While at Hurlburt Field, I learned Chief Russ Mylenbush who worked with me in the 33rd OSS at Eglin was in charge of the F-15 simulators at the 33rd Fighter Wing. I called Russ and set up a time for Rolly and me to fly the simulators. These complex training devices are remarkable. The cockpits are exact copies of the real thing and all the gadgets and gizmos work like the real thing.

It's shaped like a large shoebox and when the rear of the box slid forward to close, the visual HD image turns on and the inside corners of the box disappear. Since there were four simulators in the facility, the other two simulators contained contract simulator instructors. All four jets were on the runway ready to go at Eglin. The plan was simple. We'd all take off and we'd each take a cardinal direction, fly out ten miles and then return to Eglin where we'd all merge. At the merge, fight's on would be called and the 1v1v1v1 would commence. The last man alive won. Poor Rolly, I hadn't flown the Eagle in a while but flying ten miles out and ten miles back was child's play, and at least I knew how to operate the radar and other the goodies on the jet. Rolly would needed help locating the compass and navigation switches to get ten miles out and back. He was coached a lot and we were all one frequency so I'd be able to hear what was going on and add my two cents which I did often. This was going to be fun. I chose to go north; that way, I'd be able to see ground (mostly water)references on my way back south toward Eglin; since the sun is always generally in the southern sky in the northern hemisphere, at the merge I could turn east or west)and still use the sun to my advantage. I was able to find all three opponents on radar and with some switchology I remembered, I determined that Rolly had gone south. So we would meet beak to beak over Eglin, if he remembered to turnaround after ten miles and didn't continue on to Venezuela. I just hoped the others stayed out of our way and didn't pop Rolly before I could get to him. I climbed so at least everyone would be isolated below me. Shortly after the merge, I killed one of the contractors and concentrated on Rolly who was getting a play-by-play on my position from the simulator console operator. The other contractor wasn't an immediate threat so I went after Rolly who was flailing at low altitude sight-seeing over Fort Walton Beach, probably trying to find his house. I rolled in on him and locked him up with my radar hoping that the Radar Warning Receiver (RWR) going off would cause him to panic and crash into his house. Hopefully Barb wasn't home. Maybe she and Shirley had gone on one of their long walks to discuss life with teenagers again. As I was turning directly behind Rolly about a thousand feet back, I selected my gun placing the pipper on one of his engines but before I pulled the trigger; Betty said, "Warning, engine fire, left." Yep; the left engine fire light was lit and the left FTIT (fan turbine inlet temperature) gauge was pegged. Dang! The guy at the console was playing dial-a-disaster with me. I quickly went through the procedure to shut down the left engine and blew the fire bottle to extinguish the simulated flames. Fortunately I had the runway in sight so I played the game by switching to tower frequency and declaring an emergency. This made the console operator stop messing with my jet and act like a tower controller. The Eagle flies fine on one engine but Rolly had trouble staying behind me when I. I dropped my gear and flaps and slowed to final approach speed to land. Right before I touched down, Rolly passed me on the right. Perfect, now I'm behind him again. I selected afterburner on the right side and did my best single-engine take off. I throttled back after raising my gear and flaps and began working to get that left engine running again; but no need, I was still behind Rolly so I popped him with a sidewinder – my first single-engine kill. Thanks, Rolly!

In 2004, Janet's husband (Katie's father) died from lung cancer. He had prearranged for his first mother-in-law to move in with fifteen year-old Katie. This arrangement blew up when the elderly former mother in-law and teenager came together. Shirley overheard an argument on the phone one day and left the next day to pick Katie up.

Age-wise, Katie fit in nicely between Laura and Jacob, but we had a bit of a culture clash ourselves. Katie was unchurched and not used to much parental supervision (Which we were *very* used to.), but she joined right in with the youth group at Wright Baptist Church near our home. In no time we were celebrating her salvation and baptism. After butting heads a few times we pressed on as a family of five plus a pair of miniature dachshunds. It helped that Katie was an excellent student. I retired shortly after Katie came on board; so she got to move again (welcome to the club)

She graduated from Smithfield High School followed by Longwood University in Farmville, (Where the heck is that?)Virginia with a degree in Elementary Education. She found a job immediately teaching Kindergarten in Virginia Beach where she just started her second year.

CHAPTER XVIII
KNOWING WHEN
IT'S TIME TO GO

I became retirement eligible in 2005 after twenty years commissioned service. Accepting the assignment to Hurlburt added on two more years of service commitment.

So in 2002 AFPC would be looking to reassign me in 2003. The longer I stayed in; the higher my retirement pay would be. My only flying option would be back in the training command but, I'd done about all I could do there and I wasn't interested in going back. Neither was I interested in flying for the airlines. If I had sought a follow-on assignment after the AFC2TIG, I would likely have been assigned to the 9th AF staff (read: Iraq) or the HTACC (AOC) in Korea. Except for not making colonel (a goal I set late in my career), I had met or exceeded my flying and professional goals in the USAF.

So in 2004, I put in my papers for retirement effective 1 Oct 2005.

My hips continued to bother me inspite of the horse pills I was taking daily. Then we learned from Bucky, about injections into the hip joint to relieve pain and provide lubrication. I contacted an orthopedic surgeon at Eglin AFB's hospital on the other side of town. There were indeed injections I could take right into the joint but the relief only lasts a few weeks.

I decided to give it a try. The procedure was done in radiology because the doctor used a live X-Ray image to get the needle into the joint without hitting major arteries, nerve bundles, or bone. The procedure was very uncomfortable but tolerable; the worst part being when he pushed the thick steroid/painkiller/lubricant/cocktail into the joint; which was tender for a bit afterward, but later, the goop took effect and my hip felt near normal. Great! Let's do the other side.

I had the other side done right before our 25th wedding anniversary so I could have relief while we toured Hawaii to celebrate that significant milestone. We flew the kids to Houston to stay with Teresa while we were away.

Shirley & I were up way to early on our 25th anniversary

Since I was still on active duty and not flying, I talked to the orthopedic surgeon about a hip replacement. Sooner seemed better than later; so in January of 2005, I had a total hip replacement on my right side. Afterward, I was quite the sight wondering around Hurlburt in a flight suit and a walker.

My retirement ceremony was scheduled for July 12th, 2005 at Hurlburt's O'Club but Shirley and I didn't bother to show up. Jerry wouldn't let us. We were directed to evacuate for yet another hurricane. We rescheduled and were able to attend our second attempt.

Col McGuirk presenting my retirement certificate, Jul 2005

This last assignment in Florida beat us up weather-wise.

Tropical Storms and hurricanes seemed to line up and take numbers to have a go at the Gulf coast while we were there. One afternoon, a super cell thunderstorm parked over Hurlburt and dumped thirteen inches of rain in one hour, flooding the small base.

Whenever a hurricane drew a bead on our piece of the coast, Hurlburt's wing commander ordered an evacuation.

I hitched up the boat; we packed our bags, and drove over to Jacksonville until we were allowed to return.

Well before my retirement, I attended a retirement ceremony for someone else in the AFC2TIG. As I was leaving the Club, "Unc" Smith, the Northrop Grumman site lead asked, "Spike, why isn't there a copy of your resume' on my desk? "You'll have it by COB (Close of Business), Unc." I had attended the transition assistance program where we learned how to translate our military resume' into something intelligible to a civilian hiring manager. Since Unc was a retired USAF officer, I sent him both. Soon I was contacted to set up a telephone interview. The interview was with a Naval Academy grad and retired Naval Officer, "Augie" Ponturiero. We hit it off and had another telephone interview about a week later. Not long after that, I spoke to a woman in HR to discuss salary. She asked what the Air Force was paying me. As a Lt Col, on flying status with over twenty four years, with dependents it was pretty comfortable. I gave her the number and explained that it included flight pay and my housing allowance. Her response was music to my ears. *"We can do better than that."* Yee Haw! More grace! But before Northrop Grumman sent me an actual offer letter; someone, in a moment of clarity decided before they offer some guy named Spike any money, maybe they should actually lay eyes on me.

So I flew to Atlanta's airport to meet with a gentleman in the Concourse C Crown room. I wore my recently acquired interview suit and entered the Crown room to discover my interviewer had arrived early and waited for me at the bar. I learned he had worked on the Apollo program. [Northrop Grumman built the Lunar excursion module (LEM)] We talked for about half an hour and parted ways.

Grace alert! As a result of a two resumes', two phone interviews, and one interview near the bar at ATL, Northrop Grumman made a very generous offer contingent on my being willing to move to Virginia. It must have been the suit or maybe the F-15 tie-tack! Shirley loved Virginia and was delighted at the prospect of going back. More grace! I accepted the offer. But before we could leave; we had a house to sell. Grace alert!

Selling our first house on West Cherokee in Enid was a disaster. The price for a barrel of oil dropped dramatically in the mid-eighties and the oil industry in Enid collapsed; forcing the town's refinery to close and businesses like Sunburst Energy to go bankrupt. Sunburst tried to resurrect itself but that new company went bankrupt too despite Shirley's best efforts. As a result, Enid's economy tanked and our house never sold. We were forced to let it go back to the bank. I called the VA with whom we financed our mortgage, explained our situation, and told them we would stop payment on the mortgage effective the following month. Their response surprised me. *We've been expecting your call. We're surprised you were able to hold on as long as you did.* My options included foreclosure, lean in lieu of foreclosure (not really an option because of the appraised value of the house vs. mortgage pay –off.) I offered to send the monthly rent I collected but they declined saying any payment constituted a partial payment and complicated matters. So we stopped making our house payment and hunkered down for the foreclosure process.

Our renter was a former student of mine that had been Faiped. I called her and told her not to bother with the rent anymore but she might have to vacate on short notice due to the foreclosure. Step one was a sheriff's auction. We bought the house for $65,900. It appraised at $28,500 for the sheriff's auction three years later. With the state of the local economy; no one bid on the house, so the bank bought it. I was liable for the difference but since the mortgage was VA insured, I was only responsible for $23K and change.

We were assigned to Langley four years later when I received a letter saying," "You owe the United States Government $23K and change." At the bottom of the letter was a tear-off coupon to include with my check for $23K and change. If I could drop everything and write a check for $23K and change, I probably wouldn't be in this predicament!

In the fine print, I read "If you feel this indebtedness was due to circumstances beyond your control, you may appeal this decision by contacting… It was worth a shot - I couldn't control the price of a barrel of oil or Enid's economy and wasn't it an agent of the United States Government that gave me orders to leave Enid and move to San Antonio? I requested an appeal; first in writing but later I drove to the VA regional office in Roanoke, VA. Finally toward the end of our year at Sheppard we received notice that the debt had been waived. But, for tax purposes, consider the $23K and change income. Being foreclosed upon has had no impact on our credit rating. By contrast, we decided to sell the house in Ft. Walton Beach by owner. How hard could it be? The real estate agents we'd worked with over the years weren't rocket surgeons; I used the Internet to access county records to see what other homes in our small gated community sold for. With this information and my MS Excel expertise, I computed the low, mean, and high cost per square-foot and used these figures to set a fair price for our home. It turned out to be exactly twice what we paid for it three years earlier. We stuck a FSBO sign in the yard and had a buyer the next day. They signed a standard real estate contract I found on the web and we had a deal.

Then Tropical Storm Jerry in the Gulf intensified into a hurricane and we evacuated to Jacksonville. We watched the Weather Channel and saw the storm come ashore on at the worst possible location for storm intensity at Fort Walton Beach. We knew we would not be allowed back into the area until power was restored, so every eight hours or so, I called the house; knowing if the answering machine picked up, we had power. After three days, the answering machine picked up so we packed and waited for the word to go home. Word came and we anxiously drove back not knowing was to expect. Hwy 98 through FWB was a mess. Boats seeking refuge in the Santa Rosa Sound were strewn all over the place. A huge motor yacht lay on the lawn outside the Officers Club where my retirement ceremony took place. God was gracious again in that we only lost a couple of shingles over the garage and a section of our privacy fence blew down. I easily fixed the fence and we found someone to replace the shingles for $150. It's like; grace raining down all around me!! The sale went to closing with no additional hassles and we in fact doubled our money in three years.

This allowed us to put half down on our beautiful new home in Carrollton, Virginia where we now live.

This time, Shirley did the house-hunting with best friend, Kathy Farmer, who lives near Richmond and found the house which will likely be our last. Tschuss! made the trip to Virginia with us. I kept her at a marina near the York River and Chesapeake Bay about forty minutes from the house. Rolly lives close by and frequently crewed for me.

Rolly checks my sail trim

On my first project with Northrop Grumman, I worked with Augie and several other contractors on a team led by an active duty USAF colonel. Our task was to develop a joint testing and evaluation methodology (JTEM) ensuring new systems introduced into our armed forces' arsenals were created and developed to be interoperable, synergistic, complimentary, or at the very least; non interfering with systems of the other services. Working with a group of retired officers from other services was interesting. My slice of Northrop

Grumman Mission Systems(NGMS) had offices in Hampton, Virginia(thirty minutes away) and several in and around Washington D.C.(three hours away) I worked for a time with Augie and some others on a project called DVS-II. This project set up improved Internet enabled, video teleconferencing for the DOD world-wide). This and the next project; DNMSS-G, kept me travelling to Washington frequently. (Sometimes, twice a week). If I didn't go to Washington; I worked in the Hampton office which gave me access to the NGMS network. I did this for a few months until someone figured out I could work from home with high-speed Internet access (which I had) and the proper secure hardware and software (which NGMS provided). I still had to go to D.C. occasionally, but for the most part I worked out of my new office at home. DNMSS-G was a huge project. NGMS teamed with Verizon to prepare a proposal for a multi-multimillion dollar contract to manage the DISN (defense information systems network). Augie had the lead and I was his wingman. I spent sometimes weeks at a time in the D.C. area. I came to like and appreciate the diverse team assembled to work DNMSS-G; Augie, Dan Fernandez, Robin Lawson, and crazy Paul (I've forgotten his last name) but those on the team know who I'm talking about. I learned a lot about the business development processes as well as the exceedingly complex DOD acquisition process.

During one of my D.C. trips in 2007, Shirley's father, Jake, moved from his assisted living facility to a hospital. He was struggling with lung cancer and it was beginning to get the best of him. Shirley went to

Jacksonville to check on him frequently. Randy Green, our Pastor at Harvest Fellowship Baptist Church grew up in a small town very near Tyndall AFB. He was on a visit home when he learned Jake was hospitalized. Even though he had never met the man, Randy swung through Jacksonville on his way back to Virginia (Jax isn't exactly "on the way" between Panama City and Virginia)to check on Shirley and Jake. Shirley had been talking to Jake about his salvation, concerned she'd never see him again after he died. Randy talked with Jake who thought his sins were too many and too gross to be saved but Randy convinced him that Jesus Christ's sacrifice on the cross was sufficient to cover all of a person's sin no matter how numerous or depraved they might be. Jake accepted Christ's free gift of salvation. Randy gave Shirley the good news and she later she crawled in bed to hold her dying father one last time content in the knowledge that they'd be together again. Jake met Jesus face to face the next day. I wonder if Jean introduced them (Does Jesus need an introduction?). I was in a hotel in Ashburn, Virginia when Shirley called me with the news. I left immediately to get home before our eleven-hour drive south for Jake's funeral. He was buried next to Jean with full military honors.

So; was it A) good luck, B) fate, or C) coincidence that Randy Green showed up at Jake's bedside the day before he died? D) None of the above. Randy would call it a Divine Appointment. The Joneses love Randy Green.

CHAPTER XVIII
A REAL JOB CAN KILL YOU

One year later, I was working from my home office. Like Jake, Dad was slowly succumbing to lung cancer. He was stubborn enough to stay home in Orange Park and let Mom provide his care. She hung in there as he grew weaker deciding not to seek hospice care.

On April 2nd, 2008(a Wednesday) Dad lay down to take a nap and died in his sleep. What a merciful way for God to bring one of his children home! Imagine falling asleep and waking up in heaven. Rick called me to tell me he was gone. Dad was also buried with full military honors.

I collected the brass casings from the rifle salute and polished them up for the family.

Five weeks later, I found myself in D.C. again meeting with the JTEM Team. The meeting ran a bit long and I watched the clock. Leaving D.C. has to be timed right or you'll get stuck in traffic. I had already decided if I couldn't be on the road by 2:00 p.m., I'd wait until after 5:00p.m.to let the traffic merging onto I-95 south from the beltway clear. The stimulating (not!) meeting finally ended and I was on the road right at 2:00p.m. That should put me home at five in plenty of time for one of Shirley's dinners. Before I left home, I took down the light fixture and mirror over the vanity in the guest bath upstairs. Shirley liked to do things to the house when I travelled. This time, she painted the guest bath. The drive home was uneventful and I arrived right at 5 p.m.

I changed out of my business clothes into my usual shorts and t shirt right away. It felt good to stretch my legs. Between the long meeting and the three-hour drive home, it felt like I had been sitting all day. Once changed, I went into the garage to get the tools I would need to put the guest bath back together. I climbed up on the vanity and installed the large mirror and large light fixture while Shirley watched and told me about her last two days.

The date was May 7th 2008, the Wednesday before Mother's Day. My handyman duties complete, I hopped down from the vanity and went downstairs to put my tools away. I don't remember what was so funny but Shirley and I laughed about something as she followed me downstairs. I remember stopping at the back door leading to the garage, but I don't remember why I didn't go out. I just stood there.

Shirley asked, "What are you doing?" "I'm putting my screwdrivers away." I remember having trouble saying screwdrivers and slurring it badly. Then Shirley got excited and guided me into the kitchen. She also started calling me "Michael" a lot which she did when things were serious.

Our niece, Katie came in the back door about that time and Shirley sent her right back out to fetch our neighbors, two of whom were nurses.

Thinking I may have overheated from working on lights while standing with my head near the ceiling,

Shirley sprayed me in the head with the nozzle at the sink. Jim, our next door neighbor showed up about that time and called me Mikey. Rick used to do that and I hated it.

I have shown great restraint with respect to my brother's name; knowing full well how it irritates me to be called Mikey, Rick continued to do so well into my adult years. The fact of the matter is; my older brother, Richard aka Rick, was called Ricky until he left Jacksonville for college. Somewhere, probably packed away at Mom's house, there is a red Christmas stocking with "Ricky" on it to match the "Karen" and "Mike "stockings. They were a match set displayed every Christmas. Go back to the photo of Dad on the Intrepid on or about page 28. Can you read what he wrote on the b-word? It says, "From: *Ricky*, Karen, & Mike To: Ho Chi Mihn.

Jim helped me to the floor while the nurses looked me over and Shirley talked to the EMS dispatcher.

I thought she thought I was having a heart attack. I knew that wasn't the case because *I* was in absolutely no pain anywhere. *I felt fine.* I was confused about my head being so wet but I knew I wasn't having a heart attack. I said, "Shirley, I'm fine!" with no slur that I could detect. I heard Shirley pleading on the phone, please hurry! "Shirley, I'm fine!" But I wasn't fine.

Why is my head so wet? I wondered while I lay on the kitchen floor.

A blood clot had formed probably in my left leg and broke loose travelling to and lodging in the right side of my brain blocking the flow of oxygen and nutrients. The slurred speech was a result of paralysis already taking over the left half of my body. Helping me to the floor was a good call because I would have collapsed eventually.

My brain had lost the ability to communicate with my left side.

The ambulance arrived and whisked me off to Riverside Hospital in Newport News. I don't remember any triage or how I wound up in a hospital bed but everyone was calling me Mister Jones except Shirley who was still calling me Michael.

In a stroke situation; time is of the essence. The sooner the clot busting medication can be administered, the less the brain is damaged. Brain swelling due to the stroke trauma is cause for grave concern as well. In my case; Shirley was told on Thursday that they hoped to keep me alive until Sunday, Mother's Day. My brain was swelling and the area responsible for respiration would soon press against the inside of my skull.

I was placed on a ventilator and Shirley was asked about my living will and life support preferences for me. On Friday, Shirley came in to tell me it was okay to go if I wanted to. I clearly remember saying to her, "I'm not going anywhere!"

But I began thinking about how dying would play out. Would I open my eyes one time to find Jesus or an angel standing beside my hospital bed? Or would I just find myself in Heaven. That same day I went into to surgery to have thirty-six square inches of my skull removed (a craniumectomy) to allow my brain room to swell. A skin flap held in place by itchy staples and bandages was all the protection my brain had until they brought me a goofy-looking hockey helmet. It looked ridiculous and I called it my babe magnet. The piece of skull was stored under the skin in my abdomen.

Normally it would've been frozen until replacement but if frozen, it must be replaced within ten days and I would need much longer before I could have more brain/abdominal surgery. So from May until August I sported a one-pack, bone-hard, ab.

I was pretty much out of it for several days but I knew that something serious was going on. I couldn't move or feel my left leg or left arm. I was taken off the ventilator because I was over breathing it. I'm not sure what that meant but it seemed like a good thing. I remember finding my left hand with my right hand and not being able to identify it as mine. At first I thought maybe it was prosthesis but the fingernails felt too real and what would an artificial hand be doing in my bed? Kathy Farmer tells me it was a big deal when I finally recognized that thing in my bed as my own left hand.

I had a cute Asian nurse in the Neuro- CCU assigned to care for me named, Dawn. She looked like Lucy Lu. Every morning she came in my room and had me perform basic neurological tests. She was all smiles and bubbly as she said;" Good morning, Mr. Jones, Can you squeeze me?"(Her finger) Even with brain damage, I managed to hold my tongue. In addition to the ugly scar on my head; I also had a long one on my abdomen. These went nicely with the scars left when I had my hips replaced. I had one replaced in Jan 2005 before retirement and the other replaced in Mar 2006after we settled in Carrollton. For an otherwise healthy and active fifty year-old former fighter pilot, I sure was a mess!

I did inpatient physical, occupational, and speech therapy. I was also put through a battery of tests to determine if my cognitive skills had been affected. They hadn't. I was still brilliant! Grace alert! Many stroke survivors lose their ability to speak. I did not. My only deficit with respect to speech is my voice is a bit raspy and strains easily. I also choke easily. I was still alive and kicking (with one leg) on Mother's Day.

I gave Shirley a Mother's Day card I purchased before that fateful but delightful JTEM meeting. When she opened it; it played the song, *Still the One* by Orleans. She cried and it became our song. I hallucinated a lot in the hospital.

I had sold Tschuss earlier in the year to fund my participation in the Sail Time program in Norfolk. It was similar to a timeshare with sailboats program except with guaranteed usage minimums and no maintenance or slip fees. I checked out on a 33-footer and a 36-footer. A participant may elect to be an owner –participant where he owns the boat in the program and membership fees pay for the boat for five years, then you're on your own. In my messed-up mind we had decided to be owner members of a new 36 footer I named *Jazz man* after the Carol King Song I'd heard recently.

When I was in the hospital, I thought I was on our new boat. It didn't help my case when I was asked daily if I knew where I was and I consistently answered, "On my boat!" When my bed was loaded on an elevator to move me to the ninth floor for in-patient therapy; I said to Shirley, "Cool, our boat has an elevator!" We're not on a boat, Michael. "Sure we are, Shirl." Our church made a huge difference for me. The hospital had a large outdoor deck. Our church praise team set up on the deck and gave me, my visitors, or any one passing by a private time of worship music. It was awesome! Between family, the Rollisons (Rolly was assigned to Langley after Hurlburt), the Farmers, the Elliots, and church members, I had a constant flow of visitors, prayer partners and cheerleaders. This is typical when you buy a new boat.

Another point of confusion *for others* concerned my whereabouts. I was the only one who knew where I was. In Riverside hospital we ate in a room with a view with a view of a river. Clearly, it was the St Johns River and I was in Jacksonville. There is also a Riverside Hospital in Jacksonville. Never mind that I couldn't explain how I got down there (maybe I took my new boat with the elevator.); every time I looked at the river, the evidence was conclusive: The color of the water; the direction of the current, etc. all convinced me I was back in Jax. Shirley swore we were still in Virginia. Why would she lie to me?

Another immediate concern was the area of my brain affected by the stroke. The part you use to assess the appropriateness of what you are about to say was damaged. I've always been one to speak my mind, like my father. But then the filter was gone. The neurologist warned Shirley to expect me to start cussing like a sailor, but I never did. More Grace!. This deficit was why even I was surprised when I held my tongue when a beautiful young nurse greeted me with, "Good morning Mister Jones, can you squeeze me?"

How close did I come to having May 7, 2008 etched on my headstone? Michele, a woman in our church is a nurse supervisor at Riverside Hospital and a stand-out player on our HFBC softball team. She was invited to sit in on a gathering of neurologists who used my stroke as a case study. After the doctors reviewed my CT and MRI images, they assumed the case study was *post mortem*. Dr. Livingstone, my neurologist, assured them I survived and even walked in his office earlier that week.

While I was rehabilitating and learning a new normal, Shirley was busy making adaptations to our home to better accommodate the new me. Kathy's father and Rob rebuilt the stairs and small porch off the door into the garage to accommodate a porch lift allowing me to roll into the house through the back door. Rob also made a small ramp to help me get over the threshold on the front door. Shirley hired former First Baptist, Newport News Sunday school classmate; Lloyd Stevens to completely remodel the master bath creating a roll-in shower, roll-under sink and grab rails where needed. Shirley picked out the tile pattern for the floor and walls with the idea of making our new wheelchair accessible master bath an upgrade to the home. It turned out beautiful. She also had an elevator installed so I could enjoy both floors of our home.

Part of my rehab at the hospital included practice climbing into and out of the back seat of our Honda Pilot. One Sunday morning as we loaded up to go to church, I fell. I collapsed straight down on my legs which had awkwardly slipped under the car causing me great pain. My next-door neighbor and a visitor heard my shouts and ran over to pick me up. How I managed not to dislocate my hips is a mystery. Shirley immediately went about the process of finding and purchasing a wheelchair accessible vehicle: a Chrysler Town and Country minivan with a power ramp and straps to anchor the power chair. Shirley handled all these challenges on her own while acting as my full-time caregiver. The expense for the van and home modifications was staggering. Insurance paid for my power chair but nothing else. She managed to fund everything, smartly.

Thank God for my strong, independent, and capable wife. When I first came home, Shirley had converted my office into a bedroom for me complete with a hospital bed and baby monitor. I had fun with that thing.

"Shirley, if you can hear my voice, the baby monitor is working. If you can't hear my voice, I'm either not talking or the monitor is broken." This stopped being funny to Shirley, almost immediately. It still cracks me up.

Our church kept up the awesome support. When I finally came home; they had strung up a large Welcome Home, Mike!" banner on the front of our house. It seemed like most of the church lined the streets of our neighborhood and cheered our one-car parade.

Kay Tippet, church member and experienced nurse came to spend hours with me to let Shirley get away to run errands. When Kay moved to Tennessee, John Green, former submariner and current (get it?)Electrician took over that role. John still spends Thursdays with me to give Shirley a much needed break. John always makes himself available to take me to our monthly mens' prayer breakfast. He also took me to my Horses Helping Helping Heroes Project gatherings. He's taken me fishing and shopping at Bass Pro. We talk a lot about what God is up to with our families. The world could use more John

Greens. He volunteers to stay in the nursery at church. That says a lot about the man.

Several months later, I went back to the hospital to give everyone a rest and to have my skullcap replaced. My scars had healed nicely and needed to be refreshed. During this hospital stay, Lori Schmitt flew out from San Antonio to visit me and give Shirley a break. She even took an overnight shift. She said we stayed up into the "wee hours" talking. With the brain damage and the heavy medication coursing through my veins, I often wonder what I said.

MORE ABOUT SHIRLEY

Let me share more about the one incredible woman who made the biggest difference in my life, Shirley Jones; not the leading lady in the hit musical, *Oklahoma!* and not the Partridge Family Mom. I'm talking about the leading lady of my life and Mom of my two great kids. You already know she was part of a large Navy family and she grew up in Florida, Maryland, and Virginia.

You already know she met her husband before her fourth birthday. You know she married young (19) to and elderly gentleman (22) and moved to Oklahoma to begin her twenty-five year stint as an exceptional Air Force wife. In those twenty-five years, she moved twelve times; including overseas and back. She battled infertility and adopted a beautiful four day-old baby girl. Ten years later she gave birth to a baby boy with her Mom's eyes. In those Air Force years, she attended the funerals of both parents and her older sister. She took in her orphaned niece and made her part of our family. Jean and Jake did the same for their nephew, Gary.

When Rocky Bayou Christian School lost their third grade teacher; Shirley stepped in to home school Jacob. When we couldn't find a satisfactory Christian school here in Virginia, Shirley stepped up again to home school

Jacob's ninth-grade. She also taught Sunday school with me at our church. Shirley has a passion for our church's youth and they love her for it. As soon as she walks in to our church, Shirley's greeted by teen girls wanting to hug "Miss Shirley."

Today I went inside at church while Shirley parked the van. Several youth stopped to ask me, "Where's Miss Shirley?" Not, "Hey Mr. Mike" or "Good to see you, Mr. Mike" but, "Where's Miss Shirley?" Shirley is in near constant communication with many of them on social media. This includes many of Jacob's friends in the neighborhood.

Shirley always wanted our home to be a place where the neighborhood kids felt welcome. She always had plenty of snacks on hand and the refrigerator in the garage was always stocked with the kids' favorite beverages. There were frequent sleep-overs, either in the upstairs den or a tent in the backyard.

When the Farmer family visited, their youngest, Jennifer, carved mine and Shirley's initials into a painted table we keep in our breakfast nook. This caught on and soon every kid in the neighborhood had carved their initials or a personal message into our table. This shocked many because Shirley always keeps our home immaculate. Shirley is just that way.

Whatever Shirley does, she does extremely well: wife, homemaker, mother, aunt, secretary, Teacher, or COW (commanding officer's wife), (it's a Navy thing), caregiver, hostess, dominoes player, small business owner. At church, Shirley is a respected lay-leader.

In Addition to teaching Sunday school and working

with the youth, she also published and sold the Harvest Fellowship Baptist Church Cookbook. Each year she also leads the church in collecting and filling shoeboxes for the Samaritan's Purse Operation Christmas Child project. The first year, Shirley donated over one hundred boxes herself.

In Oklahoma, Shirley got into scrapbooking. As a result, she became a Creative Memories consultant and sales person. She was exceptional at it. In her first year she was the top salesperson in the southwest region. With the extra money she earned, she bought a redwood swing/play set for the backyard for Jacob and a Benelli shotgun for my new love of hunting. I picked a winner, didn't I? In the Air Force, members are frequently recognized for their accomplishments. We've got plaques and certificates for everything!

At the end of each assignment the member is typically awarded a medal for their contribution to the unit or its mission. They are also usually given a plaque or photo signed by the rest of the unit. At retirement, the member is given those for the last assignment plus a shadowbox containing a career's worth of medals, ribbons, wings and other insignia plus a US flag flown over the US Capital folded into a triangle. There is also a retirement pin and a retirement certificate signed by the President.

Add the RMO collection and the scores of squadron coffee mugs and the Air Force wife is left with a bunch of stuff to find a place to display and keep clean or store. That is her reward for a lifetime of service. Shirley was recognized officially during our last assignment at Vance AFB in 2000. She was the Joan Orr Air Force Spouse of the Year.

Air Force family, 2000

I mentioned earlier, she is a small business owner. I blame that on Kathy Farmer:

When Kathy used to come down from Chester to visit; she and Shirley shopped all the Thrift shops in the area and purchased inexpensive dishes and whatnot. Then they hauled their booty home and played like schoolgirls around the table. They took a platter, for example, and glued a bowl on it to create a chips and salsa plate. Add a little color or some glued-on bling and voila! You've got something someone might want to buy at twice what you put into it. Looking to generate a little extra income to help cover some of the astronomical costs of everything I needed, medically; Shirley took these items to local venues and sold them with a small card attached, identifying them as Renewed Creations. This name was taken from II Corinthians 5:17 – For if any man is in Christ; he is a new creation, old things have passed away and all things are new! (NIV). Renewed Creations were well received. So Shirley decided to open her own consignment store. She found a store located in a busy shopping center near our home and opened in August 2012. Renewed Creations Consignment Store was an instant success. The ideal location coupled with our hard economic times led to many customers. Shirley's soft heart cuts into her bottom line.

She sees her store as a ministry to the hurting. Many stop by just to talk. If someone mentions not having quite enough money for an item, Shirley gives it to them.

Last year, Shirley arranged for our family to serve Thanksgiving dinner at a local homeless shelter. She was so moved at the sight of young families with small children in the shelter that she went to the store and pulled all of the coats off the racks and gave them away, too. A few days ago, a young man admired a watch in Shirley's store; Shirley learned from the young woman with him that he was in the Navy and deploying overseas in a few days. While at the register with his girlfriend, Shirley handed him the watch and said, "Thank-you for your service." He tried to decline the offer but Shirley insisted saying," My father served in the Navy for thirty years, so in honor of his memory, thank-you for your service. He accepted the watch. Sometimes, there's no arguing with Shirley. What an amazing woman, she is! What a blessed man, I am!

I still clearly remember not the day, not the hour, but the exact moment I realized she was *the one*. We were driving back from Jax beach in *the car*. Shirley was resting her head on my right leg trying to nap on the long ride back to Fouraker Road. Shirley has naturally curly hair. High humidity really makes it curl up tight. I looked down and saw her half wet, wind-blown, curly head, sun-kissed cheeks and nose, all with a dusting of Florida sand. She was completely relaxed and her eyes were closed as she dozed. I thought I was looking at the face of an angel. That was it for me.

I was in love and she *was the one!* That was over thirty-five years ago and she's *Still the One.* (Cue Orleans!)

Even though Shirley hates to be cold and doesn't like boats that lean she tried skiing and took sailing lessons. Since she took an official Red Cross sailing course, she likes to rub it in that she has a sailing card and I don't. Gentlemen; here's some advice; do not try to teach your wife, fiancé, girlfriend, etc. to ski. I tried this and it was a disaster.

I explained the snowplow and how to shift your weight from ski to ski to turn. Shirley was having trouble with the concept. The fact that she hates being cold didn't help. My Florida bride sat down on a Colorado slope to have a good cry. I rushed uphill to check on her. Rushing uphill with skis on is not an easy thing to do, especially in the Rockies. (Okay, I'll stop whining about Colorado's altitude now.) "It doesn't work!" she pouted. "What do you mean it doesn't work?!" "There must be 150 people on this slope. It works for them!" (Not my finest hour). She took off her rental skis and walked down the hill. The light has since come on, and Shirley's color-coordinated ski gear is in the closet with mine.

CHAPTER XX

LIFE ROLLS ON

Shirley and I strive to carry on with our lives as normally as possible given my mobility challenges. We've lived a blessed life together so far and see no reason for change. We intend to keep going and doing.

In October 2010, Shirley and I attended my USAFA class' thirtieth reunion. Last spring, Shirley, Kathy and I drove to Jacksonville to visit Mom and Karen. I also met Mr. Marsh for lunch at a restaurant on Black Creek where I skied prior to my wedding.

At lunch, I met Mr. Marsh's wife who attended Phillips University in Enid, OK – (a small world moment). I always got a kick out of Phillips University's mascot – the skunk. Get it? Skunks - PU.

On Friday of this week, Heembo is flying here to drive me to the U.S. Sailboat Show in Annapolis, MD.

Shirley's outstanding efforts making our home and vehicle accessible helps immeasurably. We don't let minor obstacles hold us back. My physical therapy helped give me the strength and techniques to walk short distances with a quad-cane or climb stairs; if we find ourselves in a less than accommodating situation. I have a care-giver come in three times a week to help with showers and nails and errands I can run. Sadie, who cared for me at the

Chamberlin, took me to our neighborhood pool as often as weather permitted. She also arranged a fishing trip out on Hampton Roads.

Two weeks ago I participated in "They Will Surf, Again" sponsored by Life Rolls On. I astonished my kids when entertainer, Jason Mraz, who volunteers with the program, jumped up on the foot of my board to paddle me onto the wave I road all the way in. Unfortunately, I had no clue the guy at my feet was famous.

Rob built a ramp for me to be able to get into their home. Rob and Kathy live a little over an hour away near Richmond. Their home is a nice place for us to get away.

Our Sunday school class has another member, Keith Armstrong, who is also confined to a wheel chair. It is truly amazing and inspiring to see what he does from his chair. He built his own ramp into his house. To keep it from being too steep, it makes several turns around his garage and an antique Milk Truck he has restored. Keith drives himself anywhere he wants to go and is as active in our church as anyone. But enough about Keith, this book is about me!

Since our home is wheelchair friendly, we (Shirley) host many extracurricular Sunday school activities. A favorite for many is our Friday evening Game night. Everyone arrives at sevenish. I select the music for the evening - usually the Carpenters (Who doesn't like them?) I (Shirley) also control the volume. Our primary game is Mexican Train Dominoes. We play, we snack, and we laugh – a lot. Two families have teenagers who play with us. They keep their smart phones at the ready to Google any questions that arise. When I moved to the Chamberlin, Friday game night moved here too. Why did I move to the Chamberlin? Did something else happen to me?

No, it was Shirley's turn.

In June 2013 as I watched television in our upstairs den. Shirley lay down on the sofa in our bedroom for a Sunday afternoon nap. She woke up with a severe, debilitating, headache. It was so painful that sitting up disoriented her. She knew something serious was up so she called for me and dialed 911. I summoned Jacob to help.

Shirley's head hurt so badly she had to crawl on her hands and knees into the elevator. EMS showed up shortly after we arrived downstairs. Shirley crawled out and they checked her vitals on the floor of our hearth room, which were good. Thank God! One EMS-responder tried to convince Shirley she was having a migraine and suggested she deal with it and see her doctor the next day. Shirley insisted something else was going on and she needed to get to an ER. When Shirley needs to, she can be very convincing with just a look. (Right, Rolly?) Shirley employed THE LOOK and off we went to the ER. They didn't like what they saw so off we went again with lights flashing and siren wailing to Norfolk General Hospital. Jacob drove me in the van. After more CT scans, she was admitted to the Neuro-CCU.

She had developed a bleed in her brain. The pain was caused by the pooled blood sloshing around. We learned that blood is corrosive to brain matter so finding the source of the bleed and stopping it quickly was of the utmost importance. Fortunately, surgery wasn't required. She was monitored closely because this was a very serious condition which killed many before they could reach an ER. Randy and a group from church arrived in no time. Kathy was there quickly too, we found a private place to gather and pray. Shirley wouldn't be out of the woods for twenty-four hours. She wound up spending ten days in the Neuro-CCU.

During this time our Sunday school class really walked the walk. Not only did they provide Jacob and me three meals a day, but they had someone help me dress in the mornings, and get in bed at night. They also made sure I took my many medications on time. And they even ran Shirley's store. Rolly and Barb visited frequently. Kathy ferried me back and forth to the hospital. After ten days they considered Shirley's release. They had determined the bleed was caused by the thinning of blood vessel walls due to stress.

Being a small business owner, mother of a high school senior and full-time care-giver was too much. They didn't want to release her until something was done about all the stuff on her plate. We tasked Katie to find an assisted living facility in the area for me. She found the Chamberlin Hotel, a Senior Living facility with various levels of in-home care available.

The Chamberlin

The Chamberlin became the perfect place for me while Shirley decompressed.

Several Days later, our Sunday school class driving a small fleet of trucks and trailers came to the house to load the furniture I needed. We all drove over to my new water-front apartment together and moved me in a few days before our thirty-third anniversary in June 2013.

The Chamberlin sits on Fort Monroe which was built on Old Point Comfort at the southernmost end of the Virginia peninsula. The Chamberlin was once a luxury hotel hosting society's elite like Edgar Allen Poe who wrote one of his works here. I find it interesting that we have a "Poe Library off the grand lobby but there is nothing by Poe in it.

Later the rooms were converted to apartments; each with a fantastic view of Hampton Roads. I enjoy eavesdropping on the other residents, many of whom are in their eighties and nineties. I hear a lot of "Back in the Day" stories and references to "the war" (WWII). These people have been around the block! I have Physical, occupational and speech therapies in house.

Today, God gave me his gift of the shimmering water again but this time he added white contrails across the bright blue sky; and a sailboat on the eastern horizon. Then he tossed in a fast-attack submarine heading out to the Atlantic followed shortly by an aircraft carrier. Now He's showing off! Seventy degrees; bright warm sunshine balanced by a cool breeze off the shimmering water and low humidity. What a morning!

CHAPTER XXII
THE TRUTH ABOUT FIGHTER PILOTS

In his book, *FIGHTER PILOT: MISADVENTURES BEYOND THE SOUND BARRIER*, RAAF (Australian) F-18 pilot "Serge" Tucker quipped:

> Dad, when I grow up, I want to be a fighter Pilot!
> You can't do both, son.

Forget the stereotypes depicted by Hollywood. Forget Maverick, Goose and the rest of the characters from *Top Gun* or *The Great Santini.*

We don't sing to strange women in bars or follow them into the ladies room. We do not stand around sizing each other up trying to figure out who is the best pilot. We are a competitive bunch, though. This is a result of having to compete for the privilege to fly fighters and the intense scrutiny we're under when we take on that responsibility. Everything done and said in the jet is video-taped and scrutinized to the nth degree.

The F-15 community is notorious for our long debriefings. We review everything in detail searching for a better way to execute a particular tactic, maneuver, or radio call. Every shot is reviewed from pickle throughout the missile's time of flight to determine if it was valid and resulted in a kill. Each shot, valid and otherwise is recorded in a shot log for Top Gun competition. If a kill was called but the shot later proved to be invalid, the shooter owes $5 to the squadron kitty.

Alcohol was a big part of life in a fighter squadron and frequently guys had too much to drink. *The first thing to go is the judgment to know when you've had too much.* But we watched each other and practiced mutual support on the ground and in the air. As a nondrinker, I frequently found myself the designated driver. Every fighter squadron I know of has a bar but no one can drink until the pilots for the last scheduled sorties of the day have stepped to fly. The rules concerning alcohol use and flying are followed.

Reputations (important in the small fighter community) are built as soon as you arrive. As a new guy, you want to establish yourself as a good, solid wingman quickly. This leads to an early upgrade to flight lead and the opportunity to go on more TDYs to great flying venues like Red Flag. Participating in extracurricular activities, like crud or roof-stomping, is a must for team building.

There are practices you must master quickly. One is the dollar bill game. It is used to determine who pays for the first round of refreshments or accomplishes some other undesirable task. The object is *not* to win because the winner loses. Another practice is the RMO (round metal object). Each unit typically procures a commemorative RMO which a member should have on his person at all times. Any other unit member can initiate a RMO check at any time by displaying his RMO or saying, (academic situation)" Coin Check!" If caught without an RMO, the offender pays the penalty established by the unit.

If everyone present has their RMO, the challenger is penalized. Inadvertently saying or displaying the C-word constitutes a challenge.

It seems every time Shirley and I dine with the Rollisons; my Wolfhound or AFC2TIG RMO somehow accidentally drops on the table.

Shirley and I attended Rolly's retirement ceremony several months ago. In the middle of his speech, I held a Wolfhound RMO out in the center aisle where he couldn't miss it. He acknowledged my RMO check with eye contact and a brief smile. He did well to keep a straight face and continue his speech without a hitch but it cost him later.

Too often, I saw young guys trying to live up to the Hollywood stereotype; with regard to excessive alcohol consumption and wild behavior. I never understood why these Type-A people who had to be in complete control of their faculties to get to and remain in a fighter cockpit, sought to drink to the point of being out of control. It just wasn't necessary.

I also witnessed the "What happens TDY, stays TDY" mindset among some married guys, but this was rare. Above all, we liked to have fun. The fighter pilots I knew were some of the funniest people I met. Maj Gen (two-stars) Cliver, the USAFE Director of Operations attended our 32 AOS Christmas party one year. Each flight in the squadron was challenged to present a top-ten list of things we didn't want to find in our stockings.

As the combat operations flight commander, I was responsible to read the list my flight put together. The number one thing we didn't want to find in our stocking was a deceased insect (academic situation: dead bug). As soon as I finished saying those words; all the men in the room, including general Cliver (who was no spring chicken), hit the floor on their backs, arms and legs extended vertically. (It's an *Animal House* thing.) When deployed to Vicenza, Italy, the squadron was having dinner at the pizzeria in the basement of our hotel when someone uttered those words and we all hit the floor. The Italians looked at us like we had lost our minds! It was hilarious.

My first TDY with the 48th was to an Air National Guard Base not too far from Detroit. Our hotel was across the street from Tiger Stadium. One night was military appreciation night. Military members wearing uniforms were admitted free. The only uniforms we had were our flight suits; so we put on our bags, walked across the street, and enjoyed the ball game. On a TDY to Nellis AFB near Las Vegas, we all wore Frito's nametag when we went to dinner at the O'Club, in case things got rowdy. We had 20 or so made just for this trip. After our meal, the dollar bill game decided who was celebrating a birthday and we began singing to him. On that same trip, we found a paintball facility and had a great time inflicting serious pain on each other. Being shot by a paintball hurts enough that you defend yourself like it's the real thing.

One of my favorite practices in a fighter squadron was the douffer book. This book chronicled the bufoonerous acts of anyone in the squadron.

The entries were brutal, mostly true, and almost always hilarious. Basically, nothing was out of bounds and rank protected no one from a good write-up. Military pilots in general and fighter pilots in particular are very intelligent people. Boomer, a pilot in the 48th was an

MIT graduate. He was scary smart. Our aircraft and their weapons systems are extremely complex. To get the most out of them, we're required to know the science behind how they work.

Tracking distant maneuvering bandits while monitoring the status of the missiles you shot at them while defending against shots they took at you while keeping track of your wingman and/or the assets you are protecting can be overwhelming.

Probably the most laughable part of the movie *Top Gun* is the scene where Charlie asks Maverick, "What were you thinking?" Maverick responded with, "Up there, there's no time to think. *If you think – you're dead.* In the real world, right about the time your brain approaches overload dealing with everything that's going on, Betty chimes in with a pleasant, "Bingo fuel." *If you stop thinking – you're dead,* even in training. That's why the voice warning system uses a female voice. Studies showed a female voice tends to get a man's attention better. (Go figure)

On second thought, the most laughable scene in the movie is when Maverick rolls inverted two meters above the MiG 28(Soviet fighters have odd number NATO designations, so there is noMiG-28)The aircraft stunt double for the nonexistent MiG was a T-38 painted black.

The tails on both the T-38 and the F-14 are taller than six and a half feet. There is no way to fly those jets canopy to canopy as depicted in the movie without the tails hitting each other.

On third thought, the most laughable scene is when Maverick enters a flat spin and "takes it out to sea." By definition, a spin is loss of controlled flight. You don't take them anywhere. You ride them down and recover from it or the ground will execute the recovery. NAS Miramar is in the desert. How did that ocean suddenly appear for the dynamic duo to splash down in? And how did that rescue helo get on scene so fast?

Military members in general are very patriotic. This is especially true for those whose skill sets and assigned units put them in harm's way.

CHAPTER XXII
PARTING THOUGHTS

- Don't be fooled like me! It's called an autobiography but there's nothing auto about it. You have to write it yourself. If someone else writes it, it's called a biography. They should switch those terms around. I think everyone with children should write an autobiography. I wish my parents had. Everyone doesn't need to invest six months and almost73, 000 words to the effort; nor does everyone need to have their story published, but what a treasure for your family.

- Why is it; we park on driveways and drive on parkways?

- Why does Georgia have a National Guard? Are they afraid Alabama is going to attack? It makes you wonder what a redneck arms race would look like. Take it away, Jeff Foxworthy.

- - Why is it that the one time I don't make sure the cap is tight before I shake the Catsup bottle is the time I wear a white shirt to lunch?

- Pastor John Hagee said: Love at first sight is often cured by a second look.

- Is there a problem with a professing Christian(like me) making a career in the business of killing?(like I did) That's a good question and one I considered as I waded into the Air Force and particularly, the fighter world. Here's what I came up with:

1. Throughout the Old Testament; God used military men to accomplish His will and purposes, the most notable being Joshua. Israel had to fight their way into the Promised Land and God appointed Joshua to lead them. Joshua or Yehua is Hebrew for the Greek name; Jesus, It means the Lord saves. Once established in what we know today as Palestine (The Romans gave it that name after thy sacked Jerusalem and destroyed the Temple under the emperor Titus, in 70 A.D,) God used men like Kings Saul and David as warriors to defeat aggressors. He also used reluctant men with insignificant backgrounds (*like me*), namely, Gideon to lead Israel's armies to great victories in Israel's defense.

2. In the New Testament; a Roman Centurion (commander of 100) came to Jesus and asked Him to miraculously heal his servant just by commanding that it be so. The pagan Roman showed remarkable faith and humility in this request and an astonished Jesus healed his servant without hesitation or regard for the man's occupation. (Matthew, 8:5)

    One of the first non-Jewish converts to Christianity was another Roman centurion named Cornelius, led to faith in Christ by Peter. (Acts, 10)

3. The Commandment; Thou shall not kill, is better rendered: Thou shall not murder. Therefore, Killing in the defense of my nation is not murder. But killing a baby because she is unwanted or inconvenient is. That's why my kill calls during the fight at Long Arrow didn't go: "Fox 2, murder, the southbound F-16 at seven thousand."

4. As Christians, we are tasked to be salt and light to the world, specifically, those in our sphere of influence. Wouldn't the best place for Christian-principled men to have influence be with those who wield lethal force and practice violence as an occupation? I think so.

5. As I read the Psalms this morning I came across this remarkable verse which speaks to this topic:
   Praise be to the Lord, my Rock, who trains my hands for war, my fingers for battle. (Psalms 144:1, NIV) What a powerful and applicable verse for the fighter pilot; especially the F-15 pilot who uses his hands to fly the jet and his fingers to operate the weapons systems. (Playing the piccolo)

Every finger on the left hand has a switch or button assigned to it on the throttle quadrant. The left thumb has four! The stick grip has three switches or buttons and a trigger. The left middle finger is tasked to operate a button that functions like a mouse to move a cursor on the radar screen. Most of these buttons move in multiple directions to activate different functions; for example, the button assigned to the right thumb can be pressed down, pulled back, or bumped forward. Directing some of the radar functions requires activating some of these switches or buttons in a specific sequence within a specified amount of time.

- What is the only US State mentioned in the Bible? Arkansas: (Genesis 8:13, NIV) – Noah then removed the covering from the *ark and saw*...

- During a message emphasizing the completed work and abundant grace displayed by Christ's sacrificial death on the cross, completely wiping out our sin debt (past, present, and future) Pastor Creflo Dollar said words to this effect:

- Dinner has been bought and paid for; it's on the table, all you have to do is show up and eat! So according to this example; there *is* something we must do. Yes, I've stressed that grace is Christ doing everything while we do nothing but that is not the whole truth. To my understanding; the whole truth is this:

- God's unfathomable love for us manifest in his sending his son to live among us and die a gruesome, horrible death in our place *demands a response*. How are we to respond? The Bible clearly teaches that God wants us to accept His gracious offer of salvation. (II Peter 3:9) How do we do that? Through prayer. We talk to Him and agree that we are sinners in need of the savior He provided. Then ask to be forgiven of your sins.

- Pastor Dollar put it succinctly and eloquently when he said we should respond with *"I believe!"* and *"Thank you!"* If you do this in faith, believing God will remove your sin debt, as far as the east is from the west. (Psalms 103: 12) through the completed work of Christ on the cross then you will inherit eternal life in heaven with God.

- If you just prayed that prayer, welcome to the family! Your faith has justified you and made you righteous. (put in right standing with God) Justification is an event; a one- time occurrence with eternal consequences.

- The *process* of sanctification comes next. This is the process by which we conform ourselves to Christ's likeness. This is what *Christian* means. (Christ-like) The process begins at our salvation (now if you prayed the prayer) and continues until our resurrection at Christ's' return or the Rapture.

- Upon receiving Christ as Savior, the Holy Spirit takes up residence in us. He helps immensely with the sanctification process. No doubt, you've heard the phrase applied to Christ as being Lord and Savior. Too often believers cling to the justifying work of Jesus as savior but fail to fully embrace the sanctification process involved with following Jesus as Lord. It's like they've got their ticket to heaven (fire insurance) and that's good enough.

- But it's not. As Christians we are called, equipped, and enabled to live differently than unbelievers. (Titus 2:11) Like the name of Shirley's store declares: we are *new creations*. (II Corinthians 5:17)We have God at residence in us. How can we *not* live our lives differently? Being a Christian isn't about following rules, regulations, behavior, and customs; that's religion. *Christianity isn't a religion,* it's a relationship.

That sounds cliché like a bumper sticker but it's absolutely true. I was convicted when the Lord led me to this verse yesterday: The only thing that counts is faith expressing itself through love. (Galatians 5:6, NIV) The Apostle Paul was admonishing the church at Galatia that had members whom were returning to follow the Old Covenant Law of Moses (circumcision, dietary restrictions, etc.) for reconciliation with God rather than rest in the finished work of Christ on the cross. This part of Paul's letter is where the phrase "fallen from grace" comes from. After reading this verse; I have to ask myself; if I express my faith through love. I need to study that out to discover how I should do that.

Want to learn more about the Bible? Lead a sixth-grade Bible study like Shirley and me. I'm pretty sure I learned more than the kids. I wanted our class to be familiar with some of the Christianese words we often hear like justification, imputed, sanctification, and righteousness. We also talked about what I called God's omnis (supernatural attributes.)

• We discussed the meaning of "Omni": all encompassing.

For example, omni directional means: in all directions; leaving omnipotent to mean all powerful and omnipresent to mean: in all places. After discussing this with the class, I asked, "What would omniscient (all knowing) mean? One smart Alec who shall remain nameless (but his initials are Russell Hall), responded sheepishly, "all iscient?" I've added one – Omnitemporal. The Bible says

God declares the end from the beginning (Isaiah 46:10) but I believe God is in all times, simultaneously like he is in all places simultaneously. I include space *and* time in his omnipresence. Physicists say time and space are linked.

I agree. Not only does God know the end from the beginning, I believe he his present at both. (and all time in between). Right now, I believe God is experiencing eternity past (what I call preternity) and eternity future. When you speak the space-time-mass continuum into existence, you get to do cool stuff like that. Makes your brain hurt, doesn't it?

Jesus revealed this while debating with the Pharisees. (John, 8:58). He said, "Before Abraham was born; *I am*."(NIV, emphasis, mine)) By saying this, Jesus said he predated Abraham. The Pharisees freaked out at this because Jesus had just said he was not only superior to Abraham but was, in fact, God.

Remember when Moses asked God, (Exodus 3:14, NIV), who shall I say sent me when I go back to Egypt to lead the Israelites out of slavery? God called himself "*I AM WHO I AM*."

The Gospel of John is a powerful book. My Sunday school class is studying it this quarter. It begins with the New Testament creation story where John reveals that Jesus created everything. There's a Christian song out now that has this line in it: "My future is a memory to you." This is what I'm suggesting about God's unrestricted access to time. It was during this exercise with the sixth-graders that I considered what the words; grace and mercy mean. I realized that, in a sense, they are opposites. When God shows grace; He gives us what we don't deserve:

Christ's sacrifice on the cross to cover our sins, enabling us to spend eternity in heaven. God shows us His mercy by not giving us what we deserve. Paul tells us in his letter to the Romans (Romans 6:23, NIV) that the wages (penalty) of sin is death (a spiritual death leading to eternal separation from God in Hell.) That's what we deserve for our wickedness. Make sure you read beyond Romans 6:23 for the rest of the story. It's really good news!

You might be saying to yourself; I'm not so bad. Like everyone; I've done things I'm not proud of, but I haven't done anything I consider wicked. Granted; wicked is a strong word. But remember, God sees the heart and the standard is perfect, Christ-like obedience. You may not have *done* anything you'd consider wicked. What about your thoughts? Have you thunk any wicked thoughts? Ever? You're not alone. Paul also teaches that *all* have sinned and fall short (of the glory of God) (Romans 3:23, NIV). Proverbs 23:7 says – For as a man thinketh in his heart, so is he (KJV)

Christ was crucified at Golgotha. This means the place of the skull. Do you suppose it's a coincidence that our sin debt was paid in full at a place named for the container of the primary source of sin in our lives? I don't.

Let's return to God's omniscience for a bit – The Bible teaches when we accept Christ's free gift of salvation, He has mercy on our unrighteousness and remembers our sins no more. (Hebrews 8:12, NIV) For an omniscient God; this is a miracle! How do you unremember or unknow something when you are all-knowing by nature? He's not ignoring or sweeping our sin under the rug. He can't because He is also a just God by nature. He chooses not to remember our sin because of the sacrifice Christ made on our behalf. His perfect justice was satisfied. The scales are balanced. Because of what Jesus did for us; it's as if we never sinned. Our sins were laid on Jesus as he hung on the cross adding to his suffering. I believe those sins (mine, yours, everyone's – past present, and future) caused our most holy God to turn away momentarily, when they were laid on His, perfect, sinless son. I believe this is why Jesus cried out to Him, "Why have you forsaken me?" For the first time since preternity, Jesus was not face-to-face, sharing breath with his father. But Jesus knew why. It was the plan since before the foundation of the world. How alone he must have felt! On further reflection; it's more accurate to say, the opposite of grace is working to earn God's favor rather than resting in the fact that His favor is a gift (Ephesians 2:8); like the Galatians were doing.

At the end of the HFBC worship service; last week, one of our pastors, Ronny Bunch, made an announcement that went something like this:

Would the owner of a blue Honda Accord, Virginia license plate number WRT 587, see me right after the service? I have jumper cables and I was supposed to announce at the beginning of the service that you left your lights on.

Romans 5:15 tells us that through *one man*, sin and death entered the world. The good news (That's what *gospel* means) is that this verse goes on to say that by *one man*, reconciliation(Are you getting all these accounting terms in God's plan of salvation?) is available. That man is Jesus Christ!

Who conducted the first sacrifice and why? To find

out, read the account of the fall of man in Genesis chapter 3. After Adam and Eve disobeyed God; He gave them *one rule*, and they blew it! They became aware of their nakedness and sin and hid from God. (As if that were possible; hello, He's omniscient and omnipresent!) *He knows where you are because He's already there.* That's always true with us, too. When you read Genesis Chapter 3, did you catch that God told them they could eat freely from all the trees in the garden except the tree in the middle? It's not like He hadn't provided them with everything they needed. God found them and took them to the proverbial woodshed. He then killed an animal to make clothes for Adam and Eve. The fig leaves weren't hacking it. Have you ever felt a fig leaf? We had a fig tree in our back yard on Joffre Drive. Its leaves were fuzzy and a bit prickly; I wouldn't want to wear clothes made out of them! So, God conducted the first animal sacrifice to cover Adam and Eve's sin of disobedience. God could have spoken designer clothes onto them but he didn't; because without the shedding of blood, there is no forgiveness of sin. (Hebrews 9:22, NIV) This is foreshadowing what Jesus Christ would someday do for all of us. Ever think you'd find Jesus in Genesis? Read John chapter 1. Jesus is Genesis!

He's all over the Old Testament! He is in every book. According to Pastor Creflo Dollar, the Old Testament is grace concealed and the New Testament is grace revealed. There are over 300 prophecies about Jesus in the Old Testament. He fulfilled them all.

The Bottom-line – Jesus is the Messiah! The scripture proclaims this fact from Genesis to Revelation.

-During his last meal with his disciples shortly before his arrest; Jesus said, "No one has greater love than this, that he *lays down* his life for his friends."(John 15:13, NIV) Just today; it occurred to me that in order to be crucified, Jesus had to first, *lay down* on the cross. Before He laid down on the cross, he laid down in a manger. Now that His work on Earth is done ("It is finished!"(John 19:30) Jesus sat down at the right hand of Majesty. (Hebrews 1:1-4, NIV)

When God/Jesus spoke the universe into existence, he included all the matter in existence at the same time. Remember the Periodic table from high school? He did all that. He spoke it into existence every element on the table. He stashed away all the gold (Au)that will ever be mined; all the gold needed to pave the streets of heaven, all the gold He directed the Israelites to use in the tabernacle following the exodus, and even the gold supplied by the Egyptians to shape a calf to worship.

I don't think heaven's streets of gold are described that way to emphasize how great the streets in heaven are.

Compared to God's radiant glory; gold is no big a deal. We'll walk on it. The Bible teaches we are not capable of conceiving how wonderful Heaven is. (I Corinthians 2:9) Ladies, look at that wedding set on your left hand. God created the gold or platinum for the band and the carbon, heat, and pressure necessary to make those diamonds. He spoke them into existence out of nothing, knowing/ ordaining exactly when and who would slide it on your finger. Sure, Man has become pretty good at assembling things; but we have never started with nothing and finished with something. That's the full meaning of the

Hebrew word used in Genesis for "created" (to create from nothing). God did not assemble the earth from asteroids and other space debris floating around the sun like we would cup little globs and bits of Play Dough in our hands as kids and squeeze them together and roll them into a ball. He *spoke* the earth into existence along with the rest of the universe out of nothing. All we create are messes. Think about this. The Gospel of John teaches us Jesus created everything; so when He was nailed to a Roman cross in a public place (probably on a main thoroughfare) just outside Jerusalem; He was nailed to a wooden cross, made from a tree He created. The nails driven through the nerve bundles at the wrist joints and ankles (to maximize pain) were made from iron (Fe) He created. He even created the Roman executioners who drove those nails into his flesh, whipped His body to a bloody pulp, and pressed the crown of thorns into His brow as they laughed and mocked Him.

Roman Scourging takes a special kind of whip; one with metal and bone fragments attached to the ends of the leather straps. They were designed to dig in and imbed in the flesh, ripping the skin and subcutaneous tissue off when the whip was withdrawn for the next blow. This is accurately portrayed in Mel Gibson's *The Passion of the Christ*.

It is likely that some of Christ's ribs and internal organs were visible after His beating. After being scourged like He was, it's miraculous He was able to walk to Golgotha carrying his cross. Yet through all the torture and agony He still stayed connected with His father, saying forgive them; they don't know what they're doing (my paraphrase) Forgive them?! What incredible mercy!

These Romans invaded Israel's homeland, killed thousands of Jews, and desecrated their temple. They were professional executioners. They had perfected crucifixion. They strove to maximize suffering. This gruesome form of execution tortured the offender and perhaps more importantly, sent a clear message to the public: Stay in line or you could be next. This is why the criminal was crucified in a public place; close enough to the passersby and gawkers that the victim could speak with people like Christ did with His mother and His disciple, John. And as if the torture weren't enough; the victims were crucified naked (a cultural travesty) to maximize their embarrassment, shame and humiliation. He was mocked, insulted, and spat upon; yet He said Father, forgive them.

Think your sins are too egregious for Christ's mercy? Not so. Your sin debt was paid in full at the cross. Mine too. I feel like I cannot emphasis this enough – *JESUS COULD HAVE MADE ALL THES EXCRUCIATING PAIN, AGONY, AND SUFFERING STOP!* That was God up on that cross. He could have made it all stop. Some in the crowd tempted Him to do just that; but he chose to hang up there taking God's wrath for our sin for three hours! He did this for two reasons:

1. His unwaveringobedience to His father and
2. His unfathomable love for us; none of whom did anything to deserve. *We weren't even born yet! How could we have done anything to deserve this kind of s favor?* Okay, I know what you might be thinking – Since we weren't even born yet, so

how could we have sinned and need a savior to die for us? Good Question –Remember that verse I mentioned earlier about sin and death entering the world through one man? (Romans 5:15) Because of that one man's' sin, we *all* inherited a sinful nature that requires a perfect sacrifice to purge from us. Jesus was that perfect sacrifice. We deserve to be on that cross baring our own sin but He willingly, lovingly took our place baring all of mankind's sin when He was guilty of nothing. He was sinless until our sin (past, present, and future) were transferred to Him. Thank God, Jesus stayed with God's redemptive plan of grace devised from before time. (2 Timothy 1:9, NIV)

Jesus was crucified during the Jewish annual Passover Feast. Jews from all over the world made a pilgrimage to Jerusalem to celebrate this important Holy Festival. There were an estimated two million Jews in Jerusalem at the time. I wonder how many witnessed the execution of their long awaited messiah unaware of who He was. Fifty Days later, at Pentecost, three thousand of them would become believers after Peter's bold sermon. The Church had been birthed.

In my mind, the worst state in which a person can be in is not knowing you need a savior. I hope I've help settle that issue with you. If not, search the scriptures yourself (read the book of Romans) or talk to someone better at this than me (There's plenty of folks out there.) or watch an old Billy Graham Crusade sermon. That man tells it straight! Bottom Line – Because we are *all* descendants of Adam, we *all* inherited a sin nature passed through his blood line from generation to generation. Since Jesus was conceived by the Holy Spirit and born of a virgin, He didn't inherit Adam's sin nature like the rest of us. Couple that with the sinless life He lived and Jesus became the perfect, spotless, Lamb of God slain from the foundation of the world. (Revelation 13:8, NIV)

- Make time to read the account of Christ's death, burial, and resurrection in the Gospels. In there; you'll find when Jesus expired on the cross; the curtain in the temple that isolated the holy of holies was torn in two from top to bottom, something that could only be done from above. The Ark of the Covenant rested in the holy of holies.

This most sacred place was entered only once a year and only by the high priest after an animal sacrifice and an intricate cleansing ritual. to cover his sin. The Hebrews believed God resided in the Holy of Holies. If the high priest wasn't "clean," he was killed when confronted with God's perfect holiness. That's how holy our God is. Man's sin and God's holiness cannot be in the same room together. This is why we need the cleansing atonement of Christ's sacrifice to take care of our sin problem which separates us from God.

While inside the holy of holies, the high priest sprinkled blood of a sacrificed animal on the mercy Seat(the lid to the ark of the covenant) to atone for the sins of the nation of Israel.

He wore bells on his priestly robes so attendants could hear him moving around. If the bells stopped ringing, something was wrong. He was also tethered by a rope so his lifeless body could be pulled out of the holy of holies if he were judged to be unclean. The torn curtain gave man direct access to God. First century Hebrews wrent (tore) their clothes as a sign of great grief. I believe God wrent the curtain as a sign the Hebrews would understand.

The torn curtain also permitted direct access to God. We no longer need a high priest to approach Him on our behalf. Actually; we do, Jesus is fulfilling this role for believers right now at the right hand of God. But, He doesn't return year after year. His perfect sacrifice and shed blood was sufficient once and for all, forever. Nor do we need to pray to saints. If you are a believer, *you* are a saint according to scripture. As you ponder these and other mysteries of God's redemptive plan for mankind; give Jesus praise next Easter season for completing His task assigned before creation – the task that began before that first Christmas when He clothed himself in flesh and entered our world through the womb of a virgin.

Jesus was buried in a borrowed sepulcher that had ever been used. I find it interesting that Christ went from a virgin womb to a virgin tomb.

- Ever take a good look at the insignia your doctor wears? It's a snake on a staff. The next time you visit your doctor, ask if they know the significance of the snake and the staff. Here's my understanding:

During their time wondering in the desert (Numbers 21:4); the Israelites whined and complained so God tested them by sending deadly venomous snakes in amongst them. God then instructed Moses to make a snake and lift it up on a staff so that anyone who had been bitten could look at it be healed. In the New Testament; Jesus makes reference to the Son of Man (what he liked to call himself) being lifted up (on the cross) (John 3:14). He did this for our healing. Jesus was Son of Man and Son of God. It's important to understand he was both. Jesus is the Messiah; which means anointed one in Hebrew. Who was anointed in Biblical times? Priests, Prophets, and Kings. Jesus is all three. What is the Greek word for anointed one? Christ. So when you refer to him as Jesus Christ, you affirm he is the Messiah.

One of the greatest joys for a Christian parent is when their children become believers. Laura was still a little thing when she asked us what it meant to be a Christian. She heard word on a Christian radio station while we were driving around in San Antonio. I explained in very simple terms what it meant. She then asked if Shirley and I were Christians. I said; yes; to which she responded, Can I be one, too? I asked her a few questions about what she believed and explained what she needed to pray to receive Christ as her Savior. She bowed her cute little head and folded her little hands in the backseat seat and prayed while Shirley boo-hooed up front with me. We spoke to our pastor about our concerns with her youth. Several years later; in our church in Hinesville, Georgia, Laura went forward during the alter call wishing to publically profess her faith and be baptized. Our pastor asked me to join them in the baptismal for a front row seat. I did. Then years later, Jacob asked to talk to Shirley one evening at bedtime and she had a similar discussion with the little guy on the bottom bunk in his upstairs bedroom in Fort

Walton Beach. Sean, our pastor at Wright Baptist Church asked if I wanted to baptize him. I put on the waders and a white robe; said a few words, and baptized my son. It was a true blessing and yet another glimpse of God's graciousness.

Jacob's Baptism

Yesterday, Sunday school was cancelled due to a business meeting. After the business meeting our Sunday school class met at our house to study our lesson while we waited for our pizzas to be delivered. God bless iphones!

The business meeting ran long so the teen son of a couple in our class used an app to order pizzas at 50% off.

We discussed Jesus being the light recorded in the book of John when this metaphor hit me:

-In Genesis; God created the moon (the lesser light) to illuminate earth during the night. But the moon doesn't produce light; it reflects the sun's light. As believers we should be moons and reflect the light of the son to a world in darkness. What messes this up? - An eclipse. When the world (our corrupt culture) passes between the source of the light and the moon, the earth's shadow is cast on the moon which no longer reflects the sun's light because the world is in the way.

Believers; don't let the world eclipse the light of Christ you reflect to a world in darkness.

• From Pastor John Hagee:

Three men died in the same car accident. When they got to the pearly gates (Biblical), Saint Peter (not biblical) greeted them and said, "Gentlemen, your funerals are going on down there right now. What do you want the folks to be saying about you?" The first man replied," I want them to say I was a good doctor." The second man responded, "I want them to say, I was a good husband and father." The third man said, "I want them to say, 'Look! He's moving!'"

Want to see more evidence of God's grace in my life? You're holding it. Publishing a book is not inexpensive. Trying to do so in my circumstances wasn't happening. If you're reading this, God graciously provided. He also helped me physically. Countless hours spent in front of the laptop, hunting and pecking with one finger while sitting in a wheelchair, just plain hurt sometimes, like now. Frequent breaks were necessary.

Last week; two men who I came to know and appreciate here at the Chamberlin, passed away. First to go home was Lt Col Pat Murphy (USAF, retired) then Kathy Farmer's father went home and met Pat. Both men were believers. I am sad that they are no longer here but I can take solace in the fact that they are in God's presence. While trying to find scripture to help Kathy with the loss of her father, I rediscovered Psalms 116:15. Precious in the sight of the Lord is the death of his saints (NIV).

At first glance, this verse can be a little off-putting. But as I considered it, I thought of what was precious in my sight as a father. The first glimpses of my children as babies (Laura at four days –old and Jacob at four-seconds old) were precious in my sight. Then I thought of the look on their faces on Christmas morning as they could barely contain their joy. Then I considered the parable Jesus told of the Prodigal Son. When the son came to his senses and headed home, his father saw him while he was still far off. This sight was so precious to the father that he ran to greet his son, and gave him new clothes and sandals before throwing a huge BBQ party to celebrate his son's homecoming. This is why I believe the death (=homecoming for believers) of his saints is precious to God. I have referenced many Bible verses in this work.

I suggest you look them up, read them in context and prove to yourself that I used them correctly.

At Sunday school this morning, we were reading in the seventh chapter of the book of Daniel where Daniel describes one of his prophetic visions, "… and the Ancient of Days (I love that term for God.) took his seat. His clothing was as white as snow; the hair of His head was white like wool. His throne was flaming with fire, *and its wheels* (emphasis, mine) were all ablaze. (Daniel 7:9, NIV)

Did y'all get that? There is likely some deep symbolic meaning to His throne having blazing wheels, but to me, it says God revealed Himself to a man who revealed to our Bible Study class that My God was sitting in a wheel chair! Keith! He knows how we feel! This is amazing! More grace in the Old Testament!

THERE'S GOT TO BE A KEY IN THERE SOMEWHERE

Shirley's younger sister, Teresa, came to NAS Cecil Field with family to pick me up when I flew there on a cross country in a T-38 several years ago; I gave her a complimentary tour of the jet. She climbed up the ladder to look at my office. I pointed out the various instruments, ejection handles, and whatnot. She looked it all over and asked, "Where does the key go?" "It doesn't have a key," I answered. "Then how do you start it?" "Teresa (pronounced Tweesa); it's not a car, to start it, ground crew hook up an APU (auxiliary power unit) which blows air through the engine causing it to rotate. Once it rotates fast enough, I push the start button which causes sparkplugs in the combustion chamber to fire, then I push the throttle from cut-off to idle which starts the flow of fuel and the engine comes to life. Well, how do you start that APU thingy?" "I don't know, you'll have to ask the ground crew." "There's got to be a key in there somewhere."

For the rest of my career; when I changed aircraft; she asked, "Does this one have a key?" "Then how do you start it?" I explained and she listened carefully for me to mention a key. "There's got to be a key in there somewhere!"

Philippians 4:13 says: I can do all things through Christ who strengthens me. (NIV) It's engraved in my class ring and on my USAFA plaque and saber.

Readers,

I hope you agree that I've experienced some extraordinary stuff over my lifetime. Each life experience was a glimpse of God's Grace given freely to me just because he likes to give. I never imagined I'd do any of it as a kid growing up in Jacksonville or as a high school student overseas. But this stuff as cool as it was is *nothing* compared to what's coming! Please make sure you're part of the unimaginable things ahead for those who believe. It's easy. Christ said to seek first the kingdom of God and the rest will take care of itself (my paraphrase of Matthew 6:33,) How do you seek Him? Here's my suggestion:

1. Dust off that Bible or download it on your Kindle like me. God wrote you a letter. Isn't it about time

you read it? I suggest starting with the gospels (John is my favorite, Mark is the most concise) Luke was a details guy. Read them before you get into the epistles (letters) from Paul. He gets into some deep doctrinal issues so I'd save him until later. Romans will blow you away. Are there are still thirty-one chapters in Proverbs? That's one chapter a day for a month. Why not start with today's date?

2. Find a Bible-teaching church and go! Check out a Sunday school class. These are the folks with whom you will learn and grow. If y'all do it right, they will be the ones to help you negotiate life's speed bumps like the HFBC class did for Shirley and me. Don't get wrapped around the axle about whether the worship service is traditional or contemporary. Get too picky and won't go.

3. Pray. Just have a good talk with Him. Ask for His grace and then standby to be blessed and amazed. Take prayer seriously. I do. I believe God does, too. He hears them all; the whispered, shouted, and the unspoken. I believe God answers them all, too, not always as we would have Him answer, but He has our best interest in mind. And remember; He sees the big picture.

4. I'm sure it broke His heart to hear Shirley's desperate pleas as Ms. Jean was dying; God could have easily raised those eyelids. He parted the Red Sea; certainly He could have parted those eyelids. But I bet He was thinking; Peace, be still,

little one, I've got this. You'll see those eyes again. (In Jacob and in heaven.)

5. Check your motives! God knows your heart. Your desire to have a closer relationship shouldn't be based on what He can do for you. But how can you *not* want to praise and worship Him for what He's already done? Look at your life and consider the grace He's already shown you; a relationship based on gratitude is a great start. Remember, "*I believe and thank-you!*"

If you're already well versed in the Bible consider extra-biblical study. I stumbled on a book and video series distributed by Focus on the Family; titled, *THAT THE WORLD MAY KNOW* by Ray Vanderlaan. He is an historian who teaches first century Hebrew culture while touring the holy land. Hearing familiar Bible stories placed in context of geography and culture make them seem brand new.

I miss many things since my stroke, six years ago. What do I miss most? Not sailing, not driving, not skiing, but throwing the football to Jacob as he runs patterns in the backyard and playing basketball with Jacob and his friends in the driveway. I'll get there one day. I need to be patient while my brain re-wires itself. The Bible says God knit me together in my mother's womb (Psalms 139:13). Since this is absolutely true, I figure He knows his way around inside my skull better than anyone. I've set a goal to ski by the end of next season. My latest sets of Rossignols are waiting in the closet. I bought that ski equipment after my second total hip replacement. When I took them to the slopes, a few months later, I picked up where I had left off. More Grace! What an awesome, loving God!

After 2 hip replacements, I've still got it!

In this book as in the airspace off Virginia Beach; I beat up the Tomcat and its operators badly. The reason we spanked them so handily was our training practices. Operating off carriers is gutsy stuff requiring much training. The F-14 squadrons at Oceana dedicated a lot of flying time to keeping their crews safe and proficient at carrier ops. They also had a lot of down time after cruises for the jets to get a thorough going over by corrosion control, another price to pay for the thrill of flying off boats.

In the USAF, fighter squadrons are directed how to apportion their flying time to the various missions to which they may be tasked. The F-15A/C was built to do one thing – air superiority. This was the *one mission* of my F-15 squadrons. 100% of our flying time went to air-to-air training. Since we had the *best jet* and the *best training* for the mission, F-15 pilots have no excuse for not being the *best in the world* at it. We are. I thank God; He enabled this 130 lb. high school band geek to be part of such an elite group of men.

- I could have been a cardiologist but I didn't have the heart for it.
- I could have been an optometrist but eye just couldn't see me doing that.
- I could have been a comedian – Naw! But what a funny thought.
- Be sure to recognize National Atheist Day! It falls on April 1st in 2015: The fool says in his heart there is no God. (Psalms 14:1, NIV)

From one of Randy Green's sermons:
Jesus said he was going to prepare a place for us and later ascended to heaven to get to work. If He created something as amazing as our universe in six days, imagine how wonderful our place in heaven is going to be after working on it for two thousand years!

In the book by Ray Vanderlaan I mentioned earlier, Ray described the betrothal process in first century Palestine. When a Hebrew woman agreed to marry a Hebrew man; the groom-to-be tells her he's going to prepare a place for her. The custom at that time was male descendants of a Hebrew patriarch built onto the father's house. A Hebrew couple blessed with many sons eventually had many homes (mansions) built around a common family courtyard. When would the bride and groom move in? Only the father knows. When satisfied he place his son prepared was ready; the family gathered together and went to the bride's village. Upon entering, they blew a shofar (ram's horn trumpet) to announce the arrival of the groom to collect his bride. For those familiar with Jesus' last days on earth and what the Bible says about his second coming, this should sound very familiar. So when Jesus told his disciples, "In my father's house are many mansions, I go and prepare a place for you."(John 14:2, NIV) It sounded familiar to them. When Christ returns, he's coming back to collect his bride (the church) announced by a trumpet blast. When will this happen? The Bible teaches, only the father knows. Sound familiar? I stumbled across a video that rocked my world; a DVD about the star of Bethlehem. I ordered it from http://www.bethlehemstar.net/. In the DVD star researcher, Rick Larson, leads you through his quest to find out what the star really was. I think he figured it out. The video is available for free on YouTube for a time but it has since been pulled. Still, you might search for Bethlehem star, and select the video with "Bible" in the title. You'll never look at a manger scene the same way again. After seeing it, I couldn't wait to share it with others. My whole church saw it! It was so popular at the Chamberlin; I had to show it three times.

- Contrary to all the beer ads on TV; alcohol is *not* required to have a good time. As a life-long non- drinker in a career where alcohol consumption was thought necessary; I'm here to testify you can have a great time in life without booze. I did a lot of fun (crazy) things with the rest of my flying buddies in the name of comradery and esprit de corps: Epic food fights; at USAFA, the Tyndall O'Club, hangars at Vance and PSAB; roof-stomping the wing commander's roof at Vance, paintball in Las Vegas, bat hanging in the Nellis Club, crud everywhere etc.

The end of my story so far is fast approaching. Another tidbit I picked up along the way by reading about first century Hebrew life: When Jesus was dying on the cross; one of the last things he said was, "It is finished." What was finished? His life? His ministry? No; because He lives today as well as His ministry through His church. The phrase, It is finished was a common legal term used to indicate the fulfillment of a contract (covenant) or payment of a debt – much like "Paid in Full" is used now. When Jesus expired on the cross, His perfect sacrifice paid in full our sin debt making us able to spend eternity with a holy God.

Prophets of old often said, "Thus sayeth the LORD" or "the LORD GOD says…" Jesus never said this. He didn't have to. He *is* the LORD GOD.

Readers,

I sincerely thank you for spending your hard-earned money and precious time to read my story. I sincerely hope I didn't waste either. What started out as a project to give me a feeling of accomplishment while separated from my family here at the Chamberlin turned into a labor of love as I reflected on the many blessings God lavished on me during my life. I was blessed again as I relived the glimpses of God's Grace in my life. Thanks Again.

As I review this work; I want to make sure the right message is received. One might conclude God's grace came to me through material blessings: nice homes, a sailboat, a 230SL, etc. This is true; He blessed me financially, (It had to be God. The military doesn't pay that well.) But all that stuff is rubbish compared to the grace He showed by providing me a way to have a relationship with Him for eternity. Those nice things don't last. I sold the230SL at USAFA and the sailboat years ago. God blesses his believers as he sees fit. (As it pleases Him) Jesus said he came that we may have life and have it to the full. (John 10:10, NIV). I am a witness to this fact. I am living life to the full. My family, my friends, my church, my vocation, even my dog make it that way, not my stuff; not even a near-fatal debilitating stroke changed that. So a relationship with Christ Jesus gives eternal life later and abundant life now. It's a win-win! One of the lines to America the Beautiful surfaced in my mind repeatedly as I patrolled Hampton Roads today:

America, America, God shed His grace on thee.

Yes he did! Are you an American? If so; you are already experiencing a glimpse of God's Grace.

In Christ,
Spike

Note – No hamsters, (or were they guinea pigs?) cats, F-4s, F-14s, or F-16s were harmed while writing this book.